It's Fun To Be Your
Friend

BECKY FREEMAN JOHNSON

HARVEST HOUSE PUBLISHERS

EUGENE, OREGON

Cover by Jeff Franke Design and Illustration, Minneapolis, Minnesota

Cover photo © Vicky Kasala / Photodisc Red / Getty Images

Becky Freeman Johnson: Published in association with the literary agency of WordServe Literary Group, Ltd., 10152 S. Knoll Circle, Highlands Ranch, CO 80130

IT'S FUN TO BE YOUR FRIEND
Copyright © 2007 by Becky Freeman Johnson
Published by Harvest House Publishers
Eugene, Oregon 97402
www.harvesthousepublishers.com

Library of Congress Cataloging-in-Publication Data
Johnson, Becky Freeman, 1959-
  It's fun to be your friend / Becky Freeman Johnson.
      p. cm. — (HeartLite series)
   ISBN-13: 978-0-7369-1805-3 (hardcover)
   ISBN-10: 0-7369-1805-1 (hardcover)
  1. Female friendship—Religious aspects—Christianity. 2. Friendship—Religious aspects—Christianity. 3. Interpersonal relations—Religious aspects—Christianity. 4. Christian women—Religious life. I. Title.
   BV4647.F7J625 2007
   242'.643--dc22
                                    2006016440

Printed in China

07 08 09 10 11 12 13 14 / RDS-SK / 10 9 8 7 6 5 4 3 2 1

✻ ✻ ✻

To my forever friend,

Lindsey O'Connor,

who has shown me what Jesus looks like

in times of joy and sorrow—

and everything in between.

✻ ✻ ✻

Acknowledgments

With enormous gratitude to Lindsey O'Connor, to whom this book is dedicated. She's the epitome of that balanced friend we all need and long for—a woman who can go from deep conversations of "telling the truth in love" to last-minute meetings on the patio at TGI Fridays, where we chat and laugh without pausing for breath, clueless as to how long we've been there. (Our husbands can vouch for this.) The special bonus with Lindsey is that she's also a professional writer. She's not only encouraged my efforts in this book, her valuable "double-check your facts" input has often kept this laid-back writer out of literary hot water. With the exception of that one long season when she was in a life-threatening coma (when she was a real dud, I must tell you)—she's the most fun, interesting, compassionate, and brilliant friend I know.

My heartfelt gratitude to the folks at Harvest House Publishers, particularly Bob Hawkins Jr., Terry Glaspey, Carolyn McCready, and LaRae Weikert for not just talking about grace but for actually being "God's love with skin on" to me when my life, as I knew it, blew into so many pain-filled pieces. Thank you from the depths of my soul for reminding me of who I am, and trusting me to continue sharing my heart through the written word. Thanks to the ever-encouraging and talented Jean Christen and Barbara Gordon for doing the fine-tuning on this manuscript. These gals deserve some sort of special award from above for working with this particularly scatterbrained author.

Last, but certainly not least, I want to thank the love of my life, my husband, Greg Johnson, for putting me back together again; for loving me truly, deeply, madly every blessed day of my life. Your kind and tender husbanding has created the garden from which I've been able to blossom into an ecstatically happy wife, serene mother, and creative writer. You are my very best friend.

Oh, and you just happen to be the world's best literary agent. I love you so.

Contents

No man is a failure who has friends.

CLARENCE, THE ANGEL
It's a Wonderful Life

1

Meet the Other
Half of My Brain

My parents dropped by for a visit. I had planned on making sandwiches for lunch, but I had one small problem. I could not, for the life of me, find the brand-new loaf of bread I'd had out on the counter just an hour before.

"Well, Becky," Mother said after we looked in all the usual places bread might hide, "we used to find just about everything that was missing under your bed when you were a teenager at home. Have you checked there?"

"Mother, I really don't think…" I started to protest, but decided to check anyway. I'd been on five weeks of pain medication after running over a dog with my bicycle. (Long story short: The dog tried to attack me, and I took the only offensive move

I could think of by running over him with my front wheel. I think it bruised the dog's ego, for he went yelping into the woods never to be seen again. But I ended up with a broken arm—and piled-up book deadlines.) Anyway, with the meds, my brain was more fried than its normal state of scrambled, so who was to say that I might not have tucked the loaf under the bed? But a quick, under-the-bed search yielded nothing but a rotting banana peel and an old tennis shoe. Though we were starving and desperate by then, I decided neither a peel nor the shoe could be used to make a decent sandwich.

"Check the bathroom yet?" my father asked, and I knew right then that my folks are probably the only parents in the world who could ask their daughter, with straight faces, if she might have stored a loaf of bread in the bathroom. What could I do but dutifully check the tub and all the cabinets? But alas, nary a shred of wheat turned up.

The Hunt for the Loaf of Wonder went on for about 15 more minutes as we searched the freezer, the TV cabinet, the trunk of my car, and my home office. Still no dough.

At this point my friend and personal assistant of five years, Rose Dodson, breezed in through the front door and paused by the kitchen to say hello to my folks.

"Rose," my mother half-whispered in a just-between-us-girls sort of way. "If you were Becky, where would you put a loaf of bread?"

"Did you try the microwave?" Rose asked without blinking an eye.

"Why would I put it in the micro…?" I started to ask, but was interrupted by the sound of the microwave door opening and the euphoric shout of "Eureka!"

"Rose, you are a genius!" my mother exclaimed. "How did you know?"

"I just tried to think of what I would do if I were Becky and got distracted."

"Amazing!" my mother said.

"Astounding!" my father agreed.

Rose just nodded and said, "Just doin' my job."

Rose looks like a living cameo. Her face is as delicate as porcelain, and her hair cascades in dark, golden spirals down her back. One might assume she is as fragile as a flower petal. But one would have assumed wrong. Trust me—there's lots of metal in those petals. She's the most "can-do" friend I've ever met.

Need someone to partner or belay you on a rock climb? Rose is your handy-dandy Spiderwoman.

Need a co-captain to steer your sailing vessel? Rose has sailed the seas for weeks at a time with her husband, Fred, and their cargo of kids.

Your car won't start? Let her check under the hood. Nine times out of ten she can diagnose the problem within minutes.

Need furniture assembled or a computer put together or wood trimming put up on your living room walls? Just yelp, "Rose, help!" and hand her the hammer.

When her daughter Hope wanted to be legally adopted and take Rose's husband's last name, did Rose hire a lawyer? No, sir. Move over, Erin Brockovich! Rose researched, completed, and filed a three-inch stack of papers with the court. Then representing herself and her family, she transformed Hope into a legalized Dodson.

Stretching their modest budget taut, Rose managed to purchase and rent out two homes besides the one she and Fred live in. She knows how to play the stock market with the best of Wall Street Internet wizards. And most amazing of all: She made sense out of the flowery hat boxes I stuffed with receipts each week and could pencil whip a tax form well enough to knock H&R off their block.

But her biggest accomplishment of all, in my opinion, is that she became the other half of my brain. What I couldn't do, or remember, or figure out—Rose did...and made it look simple. She was the wind beneath my writing and speaking wings, allowing me to creatively fly while she managed the myriad of details.

Typically, during the years when I was writing and speaking and raising a family, Rose would come in around nine o'clock in the morning, catch me in my pajamas, no makeup, hair going every which way like a startled goose, usually answering email. Then we'd mosey to the kitchen for coffee talk and, depending on the amount of drama in the ongoing soap operas of our lives, we'd spend some time visiting. Some days there were tears in our mugs, accompanied by heartfelt prayers.

Many days we'd get into "Real Businesswomen Mode" and quickly jot down our to-do's for the day and head in separate directions to check them off. But we both often confessed to feeling like we were two little girls playing "office" most of those happy years working side by side. How could work be this much fun?

Rose, so tiny and fragile in appearance, was my absolute rock when crisis hit our family. Perhaps you've seen the slogan that says "Put Your Big Girl Panties On and Deal with It"? Rose helped me deal with what had to be done, giving me just the right mixture of empathy to soothe my aching heart and pep-talks to keep me putting one foot in front of the other.

One afternoon over a kitchen table lunch, I asked Rose a question I'd always wanted to ask.

"Rose, what in the world gave you such a deep-seated conviction that you could tackle just about anything life threw at you? How did you become such a Jill of All Trades?"

"You know, I think part of it was the resilience I had to learn from a tough growing-up period," Rose explained thoughtfully as she took a sip of iced tea. "My mother and father divorced when I was young, and for some time my sisters and I were left in the care of my grandmother. My father later married a kind-hearted woman and took us home to live with them. Dad, though he made mistakes, began to fix what had been broken in our lives. He started going to church and infusing us girls with the belief that any person could, with God's help, get a new start in life. Also, he believed anything could be fixed—with a little faith, some creative thinking, a few trips to the library for research, and a lot of hard work."

"You've told me that you felt abandoned by your real mother, but when she was dying of cancer, you went to her, ministering to her physical and emotional pain, and allowed her to die with peace in her heart. How were you able to do that?"

"When I was a little girl I was influenced by the words of Betsie ten Boom in a movie called *The Hiding Place*. Under the cruelty of the Nazis, Corrie struggled with a deep-seated rage, but Betsie's words to her were, 'No hate, Corrie. No hate.' I think this became my motto for all that went wrong in my life," Rose continued. "Being one of the 'poor little girls from the divorced family,' the absence of my real mother, and my first husband abandoning me and our newborn daughter for another woman all left their wounds. At each point I knew I had two choices—to let the hate burn a hole in my heart or to let go, forgive, and let God's love keep flowing in my life."

Little did I know how much Rose's mental and spiritual strength would serve as a beacon of hope for me in the months to follow as I suffered through the shock of my nearly three-decade-long marriage coming to an end. How often I looked at her life and thought, *If Rose survived what she did without bitterness, I can forgive and move forward too. If Rose found a joyful life after so much heartache, so will I.* In fact, Rose actually grew more youthful and beautiful in appearance as she aged, and I truly believe it is because after each disappointment and heartache, she consciously chose to become "better" instead of pickling herself in bitterness.

Though Rose and I now live in two different states, the state of our friendship remains the same. When I was struggling with letting go, forgiving, and relinquishing some festering grudges, Rose emailed me a good dose of hard-earned wisdom. "There's the life you learn from, Becky, and the life you live. My best advice to you is to take all the lessons you can glean from the pain of the past, including the mistakes you have made, and use them as building blocks of compassion and wisdom in this wonderful life you are living right now. Live fully in the 'joyous now,' not in the 'painful then.'"

I reread those words, once, twice…a dozen times, as if mentally washing my brain in her wisdom. Soon I felt as though a two-ton truck had been lifted from my shoulders.

I miss those days of working side by side with my can-do friend, making plans and sipping hot coffee (always with a squirt of Hershey's chocolate and a shot of whipped cream). Rose gave me roots in those years when we saw each other all the time. But she's also given me wings to fly unencumbered by bitterness or unforgiveness into the life I'm so happily living today.

❊ ❊ ❊

Pain nourishes courage. You can't be brave if you've only had wonderful things happen to you.

MARY TYLER MOORE
Women Say the Wisest Things

2

Friends for a Season, Friends for a Reason, Friends for Life

⌐ittle nine-year-old McKenna, the daughter of my pastor, is a sunshine child—a little girl without guile who, like a miniature Mary Tyler Moore, can turn the world on with her smile. She can also belt out a beautiful song at the drop of a hat. So talented and uninhibited is she that she recently met me at the entrance of the church with a big hello and a hug that wouldn't let go.

"Wow!" I said, "You are the best church-greeter I've ever had!"

"Oh," she said brightly, "I'm just waiting for Ashton."

"Is she your best friend?"

McKenna looked at me as though I'd just sprouted daisies from my head. She was bewildered at my question.

"*All* my friends are my best friends," she carefully explained. "I could never choose which one is best."

Not surprisingly, McKenna recently won the role of irrepressible and unsinkable Orphan Annie in her school play, beating out the "class star," who is several years older. She got the role not only because of possessing such a big voice in such a small body, but also because she lives like the sun will always come out tomorrow and assumes plenty of friends will show up with shades, beach umbrellas, and a portable karaoke machine.

Now, wouldn't it be lovely if we women reached adulthood with such an untainted, generous, and wholly *holy* view of friendship? Truth be told, friendship for most of us has been a mixed bag of blessings and travails.

A 19-year-old young woman was at my kitchen table bemoaning the state of friendship these days. In abject frustration she had mentally checked off most of her buddies as not being "true friend" material. Each one had legitimately disappointed her in some way at some time—stood her up, let her down, put her off, or left her out.

"You know," I said thoughtfully, "you have every reason to feel hurt or angry, especially since it sounds like you are the kind of friend who believes in showing up for your friends and keeping your word no matter what."

She nodded, relieved someone understood. "When someone does me wrong, or doesn't show up when they promised, or hurts my feelings, even one time, that's it for me. I mean, I'll be polite, but my heart is closed to any meaningful friendship."

"So how many friends do you have right now?"

"Um, not many." She shifted uncomfortably in her chair. "Okay, the truth? Right now? Not any."

"Honey, I have to be honest, I have several wonderful friends, and every one of them has disappointed me in some way at some time. If I kept my standards as high as yours are right now, truthfully I'd have zero friends too. Of course, you are right to have healthy boundaries in place to protect your heart—but it's a good general rule to give your friends quite a bit of slack. Because no matter how good of a friend you try to be, you'll mess up at some time in some way, even if it is unintentional."

She nodded, taking this in as information to mull over, and the conversation took another turn—to what I call "The Myth of the One Perfect Friend."

"I just wish there were one all-purpose friend," she moaned. "I only need one!"

I laughed gently. "I guess most girls grow up yearning for that one best friend or, as Anne of Green Gables called her, 'a kindred spirit and bosom buddy.' Now that friend may come along…in time. But in the meantime, having a variety of friends for a variety of situations is a wonderful treat in this life. Maybe you have a friend who loves going to movies, but is a conversational dud. Just enjoy a chick flick night with her, and don't expect deep chick-chat afterward. You've probably got a friend who is a great conversationalist, but because of that rare relational knack, she may be busy with a full life of other friends too. So plan way ahead with her, and enjoy her company a few times a year. Realize she won't be able to be an everyday or even a weekly friend."

"Hmmm…maybe I am putting too much pressure on one person."

"It's easy to do without even realizing it. Just try to enjoy what a friend can give you, and don't expect him or her to suddenly change into the friend you idealize. I think you'll have a lot more fun."

A candid and hilarious friend of mine named Kendra Smiley

(no kidding, that's her real name) once told me, "Here's what I think potential friends should do when they meet each other. Each one should honestly tell the other their worst three faults. If they can accept those faults or work around them, then full steam ahead. If one of those faults is going to frustrate the other out of her ever-lovin' gourd, kindly shake hands and part company before any more emotional energy gets invested and wasted."

Not a bad idea, really. As for me, one of the first faults I'd have to confess is my tendency toward tardiness. "Look, you should know this about me. I'm late. A lot. So late so often I'm known as the Late Becky Johnson. I'm not dead; I'm just running painfully behind schedule. I've given being on time a good 30-year try, but my incredible optimism (which is a plus, by the way, in other areas) continues to believe that there will be no traffic, the lights will always be green, and other people's clocks will be off. Or that somehow the sun will stand still for me. I just know this is one of my most frustrating flaws. The best way to cope is probably to bring a good book or tell me to meet you 30 minutes earlier than you actually expect me to show up."

Friendship, like child-rearing and marriage, can be one of life's most rewarding and enriching experiences—or the most excruciating. Most friendships eventually go through a testing by fire, and few remain friends following a big blow-out. But oh…those who remain, they are pure gold. Still, even the most golden of friendships (like marriages in their golden years) have their moments of failure, of miscommunication, of disappointment and lack of consideration. "Nobody's puhfect," like the 12-year-old, tongue-tied girl said in the classic movie *Days of Heaven*, of her big brother whom she adored, but who seemed to get himself into one mess after another.

Most friendships in this life turn out to be friends for a reason (you are employed together, you live next door, you are working on a mutual project), or friends for a season (you shared children who were friends, you met needs in each other that have now dissolved, you were thrown together in a temporary crisis, and so on). Very few people in this life will turn out to be friends for life. One, or possibly, two or three friends whom you now love and enjoy will be there at the very end of your life, or you, at theirs, in full measure. These may be among the most treasured people in your life, so cherish this rare gift. But do not discount the friends for a reason or the friends for a season, for they come bearing gifts too, even if they don't turn out to be bosom buddies of the lifelong variety. Even if the friendship is over, or not quite as close, bless the time you were an encouragement to each other...and then turn your eyes to the future and all the new friends who await you on life's new and winding paths.

❊ ❊ ❊

The tender friendships one gives up, on parting,
leave their bite on the heart, but also a curious
feeling of a treasure somewhere buried.

ANTOINE DE SAINT-EXUPÉRY
Southern Mail, 1929

3

Beauty Therapy

I call the decade of the thirties the "adolescence" of midlife. It's the years that bridge being decidedly young and hip with being middle-aged with aching hips. It's a season complete with all the awkward seesawing that comes with any transitional stage. I woke up one morning in my mid-thirties and looked in the mirror. Along with the sight of a few worrisome wrinkles around my forehead, there, on the end of my nose, beamed a bright red pimple. Even my hormones couldn't seem to make up their mind—suspended as they were somewhere betwixt puberty and menopause. To add injury to insult, I walked outside into an unexpected torrent of rain. The only thing sagging lower than my hair and face was my self-esteem.

That did it! I knew the time had come when I simply had to find some "me" time. After dropping the kids off with their dad for a fast-food supper, I headed for my friend Mary's house. Besides being my best friend during my thirty-something years, Mary sold a lovely line of cosmetics and was a professional hairdresser with a shop in her home. Actually, she prefers to be called a "glamour technician." That day I needed all the glam she could possibly give.

Heading straight for her work station, I stepped over two toys and one kitten belonging to Mary's children, Michael and Michele, aged nine and six. I dropped into the beauty chair and sighed deeply.

"You know, you're going to think I'm silly, but I've been so self-conscious about this little blemish today."

"Really?" Mary asked in mild surprise. "Why I…" she moved in for a closer look, stepped back, frowned, clicked her tongue. "I don't believe I've ever noticed anything that big on your face before."

"Thanks." My reply dripped sarcasm. "Perhaps I should excuse myself so I can go spackle over this volcano erupting on my nose."

"Just teasin' with you, Beck," Mary tried to reassure me. "You stay put, and we'll try some fun color on your hair. Something like…Plum Brown. It has nice burgundy highlights to accentuate your red…lips," she finished carefully. Then she set to work turning me Plum Brown.

Considering the large size of the yellow gloves she wore, she deftly measured, mixed, and stirred.

"Sorry about these big ol' Playtex gloves. I'm out of the professional latex kind. But we'll make do." Looking back over my day, it seemed the least of my problems.

At that moment, Kitty decided to make his escape from the sofa and jumped at Mary, attaching himself to her leg with his small but efficient claws. She screamed and planted her dye-smeared gloves into my forehead, leaving three extra large Plum Brown fingerprints, complete with burgundy highlights. In the aftermath, our eyes held.

"Nice touch," I said.

Mary apologized profusely while she dabbed at my forehead. Then she applied the rest of the dye to my head, jerking and yanking at my hair with the huge plastic gloves.

"I'm not hurting you, am I?" She was really very kind, and through my tears I assured her that it did not hurt quite so much as natural childbirth. I tried to remember my Lamaze breathing. Things seemed to settle down, and I began to relax and wonder just how gorgeous I might be when the labor was over. Then Mary said something I found unsettling.

"Uh-oh," is what she said.

"What do you mean, 'uh-oh'?"

"Oh nothing." Silence. More pulling. "Becky—you haven't been losing a lot of hair lately, have you?"

"No!" I fought the swelling panic in my chest. "Am I losing hair now?"

"A little," Mary answered in a professional, try-not-to-alarm-the-client voice.

"How much is a little?"

"Well...no more than you'd lose, say, with a little chemotherapy."

From the sofa, Michael and Michele collapsed with glee. "We love it when Becky comes over! This kind of stuff never happens to Mom's other customers. Hey, we could give Becky a T-shirt that says, 'No Hair by Mary.'"

We managed to salvage what was left of my hair, and I left

Mary's house Plum Brown and plumb tuckered out. As I drove wearily into the driveway of our home, my youngest child, Gabriel, ran out to meet me and smiled his three-year-old smile. How good it was to see raw, unconditional love in his pint-sized form. He put both hands on my cheeks and gazed tenderly into my eyes.

"Mommy," he said, "your nose is really fat."

It was enough to have had a bad hair day, but coupled with a bad nose day it was too much. Not even the best efforts of my best friend could put my humpty-dumpty ego back together again. Sometimes you just have to go to bed and have a good cry and wait for the dawn.

To my everlasting gratitude, when I woke up the next morning the sun had risen and my nose had shrunk to its near-normal size and faded to a color at least slightly less intense than my hair. I felt better for the time being, realizing that hey, we can't all look like Barbie all of the time now, can we? Besides I know a secret. Barbie is hollow inside. I know because Gabe took his sister's Barbie doll heads off with regularity.

The Lord has to forgive me for sometimes wanting to be like the women who never have a bad hair day or blemishes, and who wear a size six.

* * *

A friend is someone who sings your heart's song
back to you when you have
forgotten the words.

DAVID COPPOLA, PH.D.

4

Angel in the Air

Strangers are just friends waiting to happen.
ROD MCKUEN, "LOOKING FOR A FRIEND"

My head touched the window of the airplane. My tears streamed. My life as I knew it was coming apart, but I had to go on. At a recent gathering of Christian women authors and speakers, I was asked to introduce myself at a roundtable. I listened as each woman told her name, shared her ministry, and promoted her latest book. Pain throbbing in my heart, I answered numbly, but truthfully, "I used to be Becky Freeman. But at this moment, I'm not really sure who I am anymore."

I used to be Becky Freeman, funny girl, humorist, mom, friend, mentor, inspirational writer and speaker. More importantly, for 27 years I was Becky Freeman: wife of my childhood sweetheart. Now, left in the wake of a sudden and unwanted divorce, who was I?

This particular afternoon I'd had to do a television interview for a book. I summed up all my emotional strength to make it through the hour of happy chit-chat while, inside, my heart was breaking and I was frightened to the core. The bridge between What Had Been My Life and What Would Come of Me? felt terrifyingly fragile. It was as if the completed puzzle picture of my life had suddenly blown apart. I'd catch occasional, familiar glimpses of myself here and there in a few pieces or sections that used to fit into a whole. But even those were rare at the entrance to grief. So much of one's identity is melded into a marriage. When what God has joined together comes asunder, it rips at the foundation of all that is dear and familiar. No matter the circumstances that pronounce a marriage over, such separation tears at places in your mind and body you didn't know existed. I wondered more than once if a person could literally go insane with such pain.

I managed to survive the interview, but once I sat down on the plane, all the pent-up tears of the day were begging to be freed. So like it or not, they were flowing now.

At this point a man and his wife sat next to me. "Are you okay?" the woman asked. I shook my head no and spilled my guts. They were strangers after all, but I have never been one for suffering alone or in silence. My misery wanted company.

I explained my situation and the woman said, "Let me trade places with my husband. He is a minister and a counselor, and I think he can help you."

I nodded and smiled, the tears still flowing unchecked.

The man sat next to me, and in the kindest of voices asked me a few questions about the source of my pain. He nodded as if he understood and now had all the information he needed.

"Becky," he said, "I could tell you what I think you should do, but only God knows this. We could talk about your problems, and I could help analyze it. But I am not going to do that because it is not what you need right now."

"What do I need?" I asked, sniffling.

He simply took my hand in his (his wife holding his other hand and praying quietly beside him), and looked into my eyes. His face was full of overwhelming love and compassion as he spoke. "You need to hear how much God loves you. Becky, do you know how precious you are to His heart? That if you were the only person on this planet He would die again for you right now, if you needed Him to do it?"

And that is how he began. Sometimes he would stop and pause and touch his ear, as if listening to the Father before passing on His thoughts to me. For the next hour he ministered nothing but love to my broken heart. All he told me was how high, how deep, how wide and unfathomable is the love of God for me. How He sees my pain and cries with me. How He longs to hold and comfort me.

Then the minister prayed for me, and our plane landed. This man had simply been Jesus to me for over an hour. I soaked up every drop of love as if God Himself were speaking to me personally.

My friend Charlene Baumbich loves a quote from a book called *Jacob the Baker,* and she shared it with me: "Jacob was a reed, and the breath of God blew through him, made music of him."

This minister man, whose name I learned was John, was a reed to me that day.

And I will never forget the way he let God pour out His love on me through him. He was a friend for only a passing few hours on this planet, but a friend for eternity in my soul.

If you come upon a hurting soul someday and want to befriend him or her, perhaps you might be tempted to talk of solutions or analyze the person's problems. But you may miss an opportunity to be a reed that does nothing but let the music of God minister healing to a heart that can only be comforted, at that point, with mega doses of love.

❅ ❅ ❅

When we honestly ask ourselves which person(s) in our lives mean the most to us, we often find that it is those who, instead of giving advice, solutions, or cures, have chosen rather to share our pain and touch our wounds with a warm and tender hand. The friend who can be silent with us in a moment of despair or confusion, who can stay with us in an hour of grief and bereavement, who can tolerate not knowing, not curing, not healing, and face with us the reality of our powerlessness, that is a friend who cares.

HENRI NOUWEN

5

Instant Friends

At this writing I am sitting on a back porch in Hot Springs, Arkansas. It's an early summer evening; the air is pleasantly cool and the sun still warm on my shoulders. Off in the distance are lush green hills surrounding the sparkling lake in front of me like giant maternal arms holding a basin of water.

We came here—my youngest son, Gabe (now a teenager in full bloom), my friend Melissa and her daughter, Sarah, two other teen friends, and me, to relax at the end of a trauma-filled and hectic school year. As soon as we arrived at our condo, I walked outside to take a breath of fresh air and generally seek some quiet in which to unwind. Just as I began to sink into a lawn chair, I heard a scream. I looked up and realized the distress call was coming from the direction of the swimming pool.

So much for relaxation.

The yelp for help came from a young girl, about age 15, who was sitting on the edge of the pool, her legs dangling in the water. "What's the matter?" I hollered in her direction as I hurriedly walked toward the pool.

"I hurt my leg really bad!" she said between moans.

Once there, I took a good look at her leg, and at her anguished face—turning pale at this point—and guessed her leg was either broken or badly sprained. I instructed one of her friends to stay with her and another to find the girl's mom as I ran for pillows and a blanket. Upon my return to the scene of the crisis, another vacationing rescuer, a kind-faced man in his late fifties or early sixties, was also heading toward the pool with a blanket in hand.

I sat down by the girl, whose name, I learned, was Christine. I helped her shift her feet out of the water and tucked a pillow under her head and another one under her hurt leg. I rubbed her arm.

"I wish I were a nurse," I said compassionately, "but I'm just a mama, so I'll do the best I can to mother you until your mom or a paramedic arrives." She seemed grateful as I played Florence Nightingale, chatting and soothing and stroking her head, and then patting her hand as I talked. At one point I looked up at the neighbor with the blanket and introduced myself. "Looks like we are the designated nurturers of Condo Ville."

He smiled, extended his hand, and said, "You have me pegged. My name is Tom. Pleased to meet you."

Before long we had a caring little crowd gathered. The mother, having just woken up from a nap, was trying to simply get oriented. She was confused about what to do next. So Tom and I—like temporary surrogate parents—consulted and decided it was better to be safe than sorry, and that an ambulance should be called to the scene of the pain. Christine was obviously in way too much discomfort to be moved.

By the time the paramedics arrived, I was so into my caretaker role that the attendants assumed I was Christine's mother. I laughed and said, "I'm sorry. I'm not *her* mom, I am just *a* generic, empathetic mother-at-large."

As the paramedics took information from the real mother, I looked down at Christine and said, "Honey, how did you do this?"

She winced and said, "Well, my friend saw some boys come out of a condo and said, 'Hey look at those cute guys!' and then I turned to look and somehow got my foot twisted up in the swimming pool ladder."

I looked around and said, "Were the boys, by any chance, the ones that are walking by the lake right now?"

"Uh-huh," she said pitifully. "That's them."

"Oh dear," I said with a smile, "one of those boys is my son, Gabe. He has broken a few hearts, but I think this may be the first time he caused a broken leg."

The news of Christine's condition had circulated our little resort "neighborhood." She had a severe break across the femur and had to have surgery in order to set the bone. We delivered our get well wishes to the family.

The last night of our stay, Tom and his wife, Judy, asked Melissa and me out for a delicious Italian meal. The restaurant they chose was up on a hill overlooking a lake. Tom had prearranged everything so that when we arrived the maitre d' seated us and brought course after course of fine food.

Touched by his gesture of kindness I said, "Tom, this reminds me of the movie *Babette's Feast,* where a woman spends every dime she has to create an unforgettable dinner for her friends. You are giving us this lovely evening, and we've done nothing to deserve it."

Tom smiled and confessed that he had spent several years in Paris. "It was there that I learned to slow down and savor a good meal and good friends. I remember watching a French woman slowly cut a simple orange and arrange it so beautifully that it was like a piece of art. I'll never forget that orange. It symbolized to me the importance of noticing small things, small moments, and making the most of them."

"You have a good heart," I said to this man, and as I looked into his eyes, I saw a bit of Jesus reflected there.

"You do too," he said.

"How do you know that?" I asked.

"You brought a blanket," he said.

"And so did you."

With that, he held out his arms and we all joined hands as Tom offered a prayer of thanksgiving for food, friendship, and caring. In that moment I realized that tending to another human being in the simplest of ways, extending a kindness just because you can, is one of the greatest joys of life, infusing the mundane with meaning.

When you bring someone a blanket, when you calm a furrowed brow, when you create a luscious dinner or peel an orange with love—you are joining Christ in bringing a bit of warmth and light to a world that is cold, lonely, and hungry.

How can you be a friend to another today, in some small, magnificently simple way?

There are no great acts of compassion,
just small ones done with great love.

MOTHER TERESA

6

The Power of Friendship

I met a woman after church one day who was trying to survive a life turned upside down at midlife. I'll call her Pat. Pat's husband, a pastor in a small town, had suddenly passed away. Since being in ministry is not usually financially profitable, and not having worked outside the home in years, Pat, in her early fifties, found herself having to grieve the loss of her husband while simultaneously trying to find a way to support herself and her son. With no other choices at the time, Pat moved to our town and back in with her parents. (She would often laugh, through her tears, about the odd experience of feeling like a 50-year-old teenager living in her old bedroom again. Only there was no curfew and no allowance.)

It was at this point that she made one of the wisest decisions I've ever observed in someone surviving a crisis. Pat was hurting, but somehow her vulnerability, her transparency, and her determination to 1) grieve, but also work toward finding joy again; 2) to laugh whenever able, and 3) not to overburden any one person, all combined to make her an irresistible friend. And from the get-go, she determined to make as many friends as possible in her new surroundings. "Because," she insightfully told me one day, "I really do need people to listen, and I don't want to wear any one person out."

She found a recently widowed friend to take evening walks with, a neighbor as a prayer partner, a fellow pastor's wife to share a book and a Bible study with, and she found me—a friend with whom to do "fun stuff," like back-porch conversations, to meet for last-minute frozen yogurt treats, or head out on spontaneous flea market trips. These friends proved to be one of her greatest survival tools, softening the effects of over-introspection, loneliness, and deep depression that usually accompany great loss.

Here's some interesting friendship information from some scientific studies:

- Research bears out that women—who tend to gather in clusters to mend—survive stress better than men who so often go it alone. In fact, it appears that God gave us a survival hormone, oxytocin, to help us endure life's difficulties.

- When the hormone oxytocin is released as part of the stress response in a woman, it buffers the fight or flight response and encourages her to tend children and gather with other women instead. When she actually engages in this tending or befriending, studies suggest that more oxytocin is released, which further counters stress and produces a calming effect.

- Interestingly enough, this calming response does not occur in men, says Dr. Klein, coauthor of the landmark UCLA study, because testosterone, which men produce in high levels when they're under stress, seems to reduce the effects of oxytocin. Estrogen, she adds, seems to enhance it.

- In one study researchers found that people who had no friends increased their risk of death over a six-month period.

- In another study, those who had the most friends over a nine-year period cut their risk of death by more than 60 percent. Friends are also helping us live better.

- The famed Nurses' Health Study from Harvard Medical School found that the more friends women had, the less likely they were to develop physical impairments as they aged, and the more likely they were to be leading joyful lives.

- In fact, the results were so significant, the researchers concluded that not having a close friend or confidante was as detrimental to your health as smoking or carrying extra weight! And that's not all: When the researchers looked at how well the women functioned after the death of their spouses, they found that even in the face of this biggest stressor of all, those women who had a close friend and confidante were more likely to survive the experience without any new physical impairment or permanent loss of vitality.*

There is a reason that even Jesus gathered a group of close friends about Him, to accompany Him on His earthly journey. He needed them, and they needed Him! No matter how close to giving up you may feel today, for your very survival you need to gather around you a supportive, listening group of friends if you want to do more than survive, if you truly want to thrive.

The postscript to this story is that through some of my old job-connections, Pat was eventually hired to be the art teacher in a local elementary school. This turned out to be a four-in-one bonus: She got to pour her life into children, she revived her old college interest in art, she produced an income, and…across the hall from her classroom was the school counselor, a kindhearted single man with sea-blue eyes and wispy silver hair. Before long he was bringing Pat coffee during classroom breaks and picking her up to take her to school—a cup of hot coffee ready for her in the thermos on the dashboard. In the same year her son graduated from high school and went off to college, the kindly school counselor was calling her "my darling wife" and bringing her coffee in bed.

And to this day they share a cute house in the country, a coffee-cup romance, and flirt with each other across the hall in-between teaching and guiding kids.

If you are discouraged with your life circumstances today, grab on tight to the hands of as many friends as you can gather 'round you. They'll help you to arrive safely on the other side of your pain and be there to celebrate with you when your life is

---

* See www.anapsid.org/cnd/gender/tendfend.html, July 2006.

set right side up again. You never know what surprises may be in store with each new connection you make!

❋ ❋ ❋

Two are better than one, because they have a
good reward for their labor. For if they fall, one will
lift up his companion. But woe to him who is alone
when he falls, for he has no one to help him up.

ECCLESIASTES 4:9-10

7

The Listener

In a book by Taylor Caldwell, *The Listener*, the author writes, "Man does not need to go to the moon or other solar systems. He does not require bigger and better bombs and missiles. He will not die if he does not get better housing or more vitamins....His basic needs are few, and it takes little to acquire them in spite of the advertisers. He can survive on a small amout of bread and in the meanest shelter.

"His real need, his most terrible need, is for someone to listen to him, not as a patient; but as a human soul."

The book was written in 1960, and eventually the United States did send a man to the moon. We acquired bigger smart bombs and missiles. We have better-housed our way into Yuppieville and created a health and vitamin industry that has skyrocketed.

In spite of 40-plus years of progress, we are still in search of a soul who will listen. In fact, most therapists will admit they are paid $80 to $100 an hour to listen deeply with unconditional positive regard and to ask good and caring and insightful questions.

The Greek poet Seneca wrote the following, and perhaps you can identify, for it is the cry common to humanity at truly lonely places of the heart:

> To whom can any man say—Here I Am!
>
> Behold me in my nakedness, my wounds, my secret grief, my despair, my betrayal, my pain, my tongue which cannot express my sorrow, my terror, my abandonment.
>
> Listen to me for a day—an hour! A moment!
>
> Lonely silence! O God, is there no one to listen?

How we all long for a listener who will not judge, who will not be too quick to fix! If we long for this in our own private moments, imagine how many people around you are longing for this gift of listening. What sunshine from God can you give to someone by giving them one hour of your undivided attention, putting all your own agendas aside?

From the moment he was able to talk, my youngest child had the gift of being startlingly blunt. He's nearing adulthood now, but when he was 16 "the gift of blurt" was in full force. Though I did my best as his mother to help him soften the edges of his words, I must admit that I liked knowing there was no guesswork with Gabe. Like Popeye, he "am what he ams."

As Gabe was making that passage from boyhood to manhood, our relationship was subtly changing. So I asked him, point-blank,

"Son, I am not sure anymore how to be with you in ways that you most enjoy. What do you like, and what do you want, in a mother–son relationship?"

Without hesitation he replied, "I'd like you to take me out to eat and just talk. But don't talk too much about yourself because, to tell you the truth, Mom, and I don't want to hurt your feelings, but honestly, I am not all that interested in your life. What I really like is when you ask me good questions about me and about life, questions that make me think. And then I like you to listen and pay attention and ask me more questions and don't act surprised at the answers or get all parenty on me. Treat me like a person and a friend."

I asked for it; I got it. Gabe probably just spoke with unflinching honesty for most teenagers in America, but they are not quite as...well...blunt.

Perhaps the following questions will assist you as you seek to listen, soul to soul, to someone you love, providing a safe haven for him or her to share thoughts that, as Wordsworth said, "often lie too deep for tears."

1. Identify a moment in your life that was especially rewarding or poignant. What was happening? Who was present; what was going on? What values were being honored in that moment?

2. Name a moment when you were angry, frustrated, or upset. What were you seeking that you weren't experiencing?

3. Beyond food, shelter, and community, what are your "must haves"?

4. What are the values you must honor—or a part of you dies?

5. What constitutes a full, rich life?

Then there are questions that are good to ask ourselves because sometimes we don't pause to listen to ourselves and our truest hearts.

1. Am I being *nice* or being real?

2. What keeps me going?

3. What is working well in my life right now?

4. What frees me up?

5. What is present when I am at my best?

6. Who am I becoming?

7. What motivates me?

8. How have I withheld myself from life?

9. Is what I am doing right now life affirming or life numbing?

It is so refreshing to be heard deeply and to be listened to with rapt attention. However, no one will ever listen to us or love us the way God will. Here is the rest of Seneca's poem:

> "Is there no one to listen?" You ask.
> Ah, yes, There is one who listens, who will
> always listen. Hasten to him, my friend! He waits
> on the hill For you.

There is only one Friend, who is *never* too busy, never too distracted for His child. Why not go to your heavenly Father now? Snuggle next to His heart and share your cares and thoughts that "lie too deep for tears" with the Greatest Listener of all. Then, when He prompts you to give to someone in need the gift of rapt attention, you'll be able to be His love with skin on.

❄ ❄ ❄

When someone deeply listens to you, it is like holding out a dented cup you've had since childhood and watching it fill up with cold, fresh water. When it balances on top of the brim, you are understood. When it overflows and touches your skin, you are loved.

JOHN FOX

8

A Friendship Beyond Words

On Labor Day of 2002, one of my dearest friends in the world, Lindsey O'Connor, lay in a coma following the birth of her fifth child, little Caroline.

My dear friend was...where? Hovering somewhere between heaven and earth? Her body was so still, and the room so quiet other than the whooshing of the ventilator. Everything seemed so impossibly unreal. When Tim, her loving and vigilant husband, led me to the hospital room, all I could do was hug him and cry and say, "Tim, I'm so very sorry."

In her fragile state, Lindsey came within a breath of heaven several times, and two months after the birth of her child, she was still in a coma. The doctors held out almost no hope, and if Lindsey were to survive, they feared irreparable brain damage. When you've been suddenly kidnapped from the Land of Normal, your happy life now a scene from a tragic soap opera, you cannot help but wonder at times, "Where is God? Has He lost my file?"

A friend of mine, Kali Schneiders, wrote a book called *Truffles from Heaven.* She describes a truffle experience as a moment when God makes His presence known very clearly, and although outer circumstances may not change, He makes absolutely sure we know He is near. And that, for the moment, proves to be all we really need to know.

On September 16, 2002, I wrote the following in an email to all of Lindsey's friends:

> I must stop to wipe the tears from my eyes to share what has just happened—a heavenly comfort to us as we pray and wait in vigil over Lindsey, hearts breaking for her children and husband.
>
> Today I stopped in at a boutique, The Mineola Mercantile, in a nearby East Texas town. I told the woman who owned the store about Lindsey and that I wanted to purchase something special for her daughter Allison's tenth birthday. The woman, a sensitive believer, stopped dead in her tracks and took my hands. "I've got chill bumps from my toes to my head. Becky, I hope you don't think I'm nuts, but *I know exactly what God wants* for this little girl to have."
>
> I laughed and said, "Well, I've not had any words from God on this gift today, so tell me what you have in mind."
>
> The woman walked behind the counter and picked out a tiny charm bracelet, followed by three small silver charms: one that said "Big Sis," then a heart with "mother

and daughter" written across the front of it, and finally a letter "A" with a guardian angel peeking through the "window" of the letter.

"Now tell little Allie that charm represents her guardian angel that is always watching over her all of the time," she said as she lovingly tucked the bracelet into a box. I thanked her then headed home.

Once there, I wrote Kathy Groom, Lindsey's closest friend in Colorado, and asked for Lindsey's home address, telling her of the bracelet (I didn't even describe the charms). Within minutes, she wrote back and said, "Becky I am in tears. Did you know that it was Lindsey's tradition to give each of her girls a charm bracelet on their tenth birthday? Allison, having observed this rite of passage take place with her two older sisters, had been anticipating this mother/daughter shopping trip for her bracelet all year, and in fact, had mentioned it the week before the baby was born saying, 'Mom, I'm almost a double digit! It's almost my turn for a charm bracelet!'"

I had NO IDEA, no CLUE about this....

But Allison's God (and guardian angel) obviously did.

Do you have chill bumps too?

He's here, He's even in this. He loves Lindsey's family. How like Him to find a way to allow Lindsey to "mother" Allison on her special birthday—even though we have no idea where Lindsey's thoughts are as she lies in a coma.

Amazed by His grace,

Becky

Isn't that incredible? Talk about your "chicken soup for the soul" moment. There's an old, old hymn, "Does Jesus Care," that says, "Oh yes, He cares. I know He cares, His heart is touched with my grief; when the days are weary, the long nights dreary, I know my Savior cares."

This is the summary of the message of Lindsey's life and of the book she was writing before she went into the coma (ironically titled *When Mama Goes South We're All Going with Her*). When you are too weary to change one more diaper or when the bottom falls out of your life with a major crisis—Jesus is there. He cares. "Come to me," he says, with open arms, "all you who are weary and burdened, and I will give you rest" (Matthew 11:28).

There are no guarantees in this life, except one: We are guaranteed that Jesus will be there when we hit the floor of life. One wonderful consolation in suffering and in pain is that Jesus often reaches out for us in special ways to make His presence known—ways He doesn't always use when life is humming along smoothly. And in times of trouble we find that He really is enough!

Though I realize that not all tragic stories get a happy ending, this one does. About six weeks after I wrote the email to Lindsey's friends, Tim wrote to say that Lindsey was waking up! I flew to see her as soon as I could, and though she was heavily medicated, I witnessed a beautiful sight. When Tim bent down to say a gentle goodbye to her, Lindsey's lips, once still and unmovable, puckered several times in her silent request for a kiss from her Prince Charming. He gallantly gave in as he kissed her good night, their love warming the cold, stark hospital room. I am convinced that Allison's guardian angel and throngs of other angels are looking down from heaven, rejoicing in this miracle with us.

There are more medical battles to overcome, but it appears that we've not only reason to hope, but reason to celebrate.

If I know Lindsey, and I believe I do, as soon as she's strong enough she'll be searching for a pen and a notebook—and my friends, won't she have a story to tell?

Postscript

The story above lay-in-waiting for nearly four years, until now, when it seemed finally time for its telling and unveiling in print. Lindsey and I both have made almost full recoveries—she from the coma and the long, slow, recouping of her health; me from an excruciating, unanticipated divorce and the years so aptly called "crazy time" that followed. Instead of living 1500 miles apart, she and I now live 15 minutes apart in the gorgeous sun-filled mountains of Colorado. I often tease her about how she was so "not there" for me when she took that five-month-long nap. "Seriously," I say with a laugh, "when you are in a coma, you are no fun at all." We're settling into a new normal, and for both of us, life is oh so much sweeter for realizing how fragile and precious a thing it is. People who have suffered great loss tend to become bitter or really, really, grateful. Thankfully, Lindsey and I, for the most part, are of the really, really grateful variety.

Yes, Jesus cares. We know He cares. Even when every circumstance in your life seems to scream the opposite, even if God doesn't come through and answer the prayer you wanted Him to answer, His presence is hovering. He'll see you and your children and your friends and their children through every hill and valley. You are never alone. Until you get to the other side of your current dilemma, keep an eye out for a charm bracelet or a truffle to remind you of His unfailing love that will never leave you or forsake you.

*When you get into a tight place and
everything goes against you, till it seems
as though you could not hold on a minute
longer, never give up then, for that is just
the place and time that the tide will turn.*

HARRIET BEECHER STOWE

9

Mary, Mary—Quite Out of the Ordinary

I have two good friends in my life named Mary. One of them you read about in chapter 3 (Mary, of the "burgundy highlights"). Both of these Mary friends are as far removed from the image of the Virgin Mary as one might imagine, but they would probably have enjoyed a lively conversation with Mary Magdalene. They've walked on the wild side, but emerged on the sunny side of the street with enormous hearts of gold and eyes full of compassion. I love them both. I feel safe in their company, as if nothing I could ever do or say would threaten our friendship or their esteem of me. In fact, after a recent visit with Mary #1, my daughter said,

"Mom, I'll know I'm in *really bad shape* if Mary ever raises an eyebrow when I tell her about something I've done wrong."

Both Marys have given me perspective on my failures. Both were, and are, unshockable. Both seem to have eternal bucketsful of unconditional grace radiating from their ample bosoms. One of them smokes cigars, the other prefers Marlboro Lights. Both love the Lord, both found Him rather late in the game of life, and both are regularly appalled at the gracelessness and judgmental spirit of many Christians they've met. Both have fond affection toward small animals and people who have lost their way—providing shelter and a good meal for both, if needed.

Most of all, both of my Mary friends make me laugh out loud, even in the darkest days of my life.

My newest Mary friend is Mary Walker, a big, bold, beautiful, red-headed dynamo known as a "communications goddess" in her world of corporate speaking. But when she sent me the following essay, making me laugh out loud on a dreary day, I designated her one of my personal humor therapists. With her permission, I'll let you in on one of Mary's Seinfeldish observations. The subject? Hair…or the lack thereof.

Hair-Raising Encounter
by Mary Walker

Since the hairs on my husband's head have…shall we say… moved further apart over the years, he's always interested in how other men deal with the retreat of their hairlines. He's very conscious of comb-overs and toupees and other tricks his gender uses as camouflage.

When my husband, Jim, and I met Carl and Marie, it was a hot, sunny day at our friends' barbecue. The four of us hit it off immediately. They were funny and smart. They were both semi-retired business professionals and had moved to Colorado from the East Coast….You could still catch lingering New Jersey accents.

Our hosts' home has a gorgeous deck and views of the mountains behind a pristine lake. It was no real surprise that Carl wore his gray fisherman's bucket hat the entire time. But Jim and I speculated on the way home about whether Carl's hat was purely functional. We had the distinct impression that there wasn't a whole lot of hair under Carl's hat. Not that it mattered. They were a fun couple we looked forward to seeing again.

The very next morning we bumped into Carl and Marie coming out of the grocery store. In place of Carl's fishing hat was something that can only be described as a Hair Hat. Thick, brown hair sat on top of his head, heavy bangs sweeping across his forehead. It reminded me of a large Russian Cossack headpiece that some madcap barber had hair-sprayed into submission and parted on the side. It was mesmerizing, like a horrific accident. You don't want to watch, but you can't look away. "Nice to see you hair…here…here," my husband said, recovering quickly.

I tried to focus on Marie, who is a good six inches shorter than me. Mercifully, this refocusing kept Carl's Hair Hat out of my line of sight. Then I noticed my husband was starting to circle Carl, like a cat moving in on a curious object, as we all talked. Jim was shuffling around him, his wide eyes straining to focus on Carl's face, but the magnetic pull of the lustrous toupee proving overwhelming. His eyes were starting to water from the effort of not staring. I grabbed his arm. "We're late! Gotta run! See you again soon, real soon."

For several minutes we walked silently up and down the aisles of the store. Finally Jim said, "There's no chance that thing on Carl's head was his real hair...is there? Maybe it's a genetic thing? Or a side effect of medication gone haywire?"

"Honey," I replied, "the only medication involved is the lethal injection that thing got before it leaped on top of his head to die."

In front of the sunglasses display Jim stopped. He bent his head forward, then side to side as he eyed his reflection in the tiny distorted slit of a mirror on top of the rack. "I suppose this isn't so bad," he muttered.

I tucked a couple of stray strands behind his ear and whispered, "Note to self, Honey. Never buy a hairpiece from QVC."

CHECK OUT MARY'S WEBSITE AT
WWW.COMMUNICATIONSGODDESS.COM

❅ ❅ ❅

Jim may have never purchased a hairpiece from QVC, but if he did, I guarantee Mary could have sold it. Besides cracking us up with the latest anecdotes and teaching corporate types how to write a business letter, she's grown a profitable business selling on eBay anything that isn't nailed down. And she seems to always have an adorable litter of pups around, the same breed as Dorothy's dog, Toto, in *The Wizard of Oz*. She and Jim live in a cute white house in the country, somewhere over the rainbow, where daisies and sunflowers bloom. This makes her whole house feel a bit like "Garage Sale of the Century" meets "The Yellow Brick Road."

I don't get to see her as often as I like, but as I was writing this chapter she called and said, "We may be moving to St. Martin's—if Jim gets a pastorate there!" Can you imagine?

I love a friend who is full of surprises, full of life, and full of laughter.

Here's to all the Mary friends in our lives who break the mold, love without bounds, make us laugh, and give us courage by simply being in their presence…and know how to savor a truly exquisite Cuban cigar. Long live such a pastor's wife!

❋ ❋ ❋

A friend is the one who comes in when
the whole world has gone out.

Grace Pulpit

11

Laughter, the Best Stress Buster

*Everything is funny as long as it is
happening to someone else.*

Will Rogers

Ever been through a year, or two, or three that you thought you, at minimum, deserved a T-shirt for surviving? If I had a friend going through a crisis or transition, I'd tell her, "You'll need four survival tools to eventually get off of this frightening island: tears, friends, prayer, and laughter."

It's important to cry tears because you've got to detox your emotions regularly. Scientists have discovered that there are toxins in tears of sadness that are not in the happy tears we cry at weddings or during sappy commercials. When you are going through a period of sorrow, I say, "Get the toxic lumps out of your throat first thing in the morning! You know that they are going to have to come sometime, and you'll feel better after a good cry, so sob away at the start of the day. Clear that pipeline."

The second survival tool is friends. We all need friends, and the more the merrier so you don't wear out just one when you are in crisis. When the walls would close in, the crazies started stirring within, or the ache of loneliness would physically hurt, I'd reach out and call someone...or better yet, see someone. A friend can't change our circumstances or wave a magic wand and make everything right inside, but the calm, encouraging friend who is able to stay, listen, and speak a few words of comfort or hope is incredibly helpful. Just unburdening pent-up feelings into words to another empathetic human soul is in and of itself therapeutic. One or two good friends can help you keep your head out of the oven and your feet off of ledges. No professional counseling degree required.

But you also need the third survival tool in your emotional crisis kit: prayer. No matter how many times your friends tell you to call them at three o'clock in the morning should the need arise—if you take them up on that offer too often, you won't have many friends left. God works the night shift! Talking to Him or journaling your heart to God on paper can be a lifesaving connection in those weary, wee hours.

Finally, you gotta laugh. As soon as humanly possible. Even if things move from bad to worse. *Especially* if things move from bad to worse. If there's a bit of laughter here and there to be found and savored, even if it's dark humor, it proves there's still life in the ol' girl yet. You know you'll go on. In fact, in trying to get this very point across at a Christmas Coffee where I was the speaker,

I related a story about my friend Mary, the "glamour technician." Only during this period of her life, Mary was feeling anything but glamorous. Thankfully she also had an unsinkable sense of humor, which came in really handy as her life was going down in *Titanic* proportions.

One day while huddled in an afghan on her couch in the living room Mary said, "Becky, can things get any worse? My husband's lost his job. Our finances are in shambles. I've been diagnosed with fibromyalgia. The other day our house was hit by lightning, and the phone literally flew off the wall. It also hit the metal carport. Our Dalmatian puppy happened to be leaning against the carport pole and was temporarily paralyzed."

"Oh," I sympathized, "how awful!"

"Yeah, and the dog's name is...get this...Sparky."

With that, we both nearly fell off our respective couches in laughter.

So I told this story to the audience, and later, after the talk, I was signing some books at a table and a woman came up to me with this odd mixture of tears mingled with chuckles. Finally she spoke, "Becky, I just want to thank you for tonight. This is the first time in nearly a year that I've laughed out loud, and it feels so cleansing, like I'm going to be all right after all."

I took her hand and said, "Bless your heart." (We are raised in the South to start every condolence this way.) "What happened a year ago that kept you from laughing?"

"Now," she replied, "do not feel badly when I tell you this, because you could not have known. But my husband was struck by lightning and killed last year."

"Oh!" my hand shot to my mouth. "And I told that lightning story about Sparky!"

She was quick to reassure me. "I know, but you know the surprising thing about that story is that it made me laugh. And in fact, I felt like it was God tapping me on the shoulder and giving me personally permission to laugh again."

This scenario has played out in a hundred ways over the ten years I've traveled and spoken to audiences, always sharing stories with liberal doses of humor. I'll never forget one woman who was so frail from chemotherapy that she could not sit up, but she wanted to stay for the whole conference. So other women fixed her a makeshift pallet on the floor in the foyer where she could lie down, but still hear the stories and laughter. As I spoke from the platform, I could see her bald head peering around the corner of the sanctuary door straining to hear every word. Later her sister told me this sick woman gathered strength from not only the message, but especially the laughter, which was her lifeline that day. She'd only go on to live a few more weeks, but her sister sent me a note thanking me for the memories and happy day they were able to share filled with more laughter than tears.

One morning after I'd spoken the night before, a woman met me at the door of the church. She said she'd been hoping to catch me to speak with me for a moment. Then she asked, "Did you notice a woman in a wheelchair last night? She's my friend."

I nodded that I had.

"Well, she sent me to tell you that she has always had a great sense of humor, but she hasn't laughed in months…since the day a stranger came into the park where she was camping with her family and shot her in the back, paralyzing her. The trial is next week. But last night she got one hour of emotional relief as you spoke, and she laughed out loud as well. She just wanted me to convey her enormous gratitude for the gift of laughter."

I used to wish I had been given some other gift besides that of telling stories and helping people laugh. But no more. Today I am enormously grateful to have sprung from a family who values stories and laughter the way some families cherish old silver or great-grandma's quilts.

So if you've got a friend who can make you laugh, hang on to her for dear life because she may be part of your survival kit should disaster strike. Here are just a few things that regular sessions of laughter can do for you:

1. Minimize distorted perception of danger

2. Help manage anger more effectively, thereby reducing conflict

3. Provide breathing room for constructive, loving, and logical decision-making

4. Assist in communicating difficult feelings

5. Enhance feelings of well-being

6. Augment creativity

7. Strengthen social relationships

8. Abate the physical ravages of stress

9. Create an environment of warmth and joy

Tears, friends, prayer, and laughter. The fabulous four. Tuck them into your life's first aid kit, and you have the essentials of emotional survival. The only other tool you might need to thrive through an upheaval is chocolate or cheesecake, your choice.

✻ ❋ ✻

*Among those whom I like or admire, I can find
no common denominator, but among those
whom I love, I can: all of them make me laugh.*

W.H. AUDEN

11

Rescuers Anonymous

From my back porch one summer morning several years ago, I watched an object lesson unfold—like a sweet story in a children's book.

The evening before, my children found a baby blue jay struggling (and failing) to fly from the grass. To save the little foundling from becoming dog food, they picked it up and brought the tiny creature to me. It opened its wide mouth expectantly. When it didn't get the desired worm right away, it began to chirp. Incessantly. So I mixed up some baby cereal with a little water and tried to feed the poor orphan. The results of our feeding time were similar to what happened when I tried to give my own babies their first spoonful of Pabulum. More cereal landed on beak and feathers and the front of my shirt than went down the hungry throat of the baby bird. *There's more to being a mother bird than I bargained for*, I thought.

Finally exhausted from effort, both the bird and I fell asleep. The next morning I awoke to a sharp series of "chirp, chirp, and chirps."

"Look, little guy," I said loudly over his baby bird cries, "I'd love to help you more than anything. But I just don't know what to do. Let's go look for your mama." I took my little noisemaker outside and balanced him carefully on the porch rail. Then I walked back inside the house and watched him from the sliding glass door. "Please, Lord," I prayed, "bring help!" I could hear the pitiful chirps through the glass.

Within a few seconds, the glorious sight of a mother bird flew into view. She coaxed the baby to follow her off the porch and up onto the safety of a nearby limb.

"Yes!" I cheered from my observation point. "You can do it. Your Mom's here now. Fly!" At that moment I spied a black-and-white cat slinking across the yard. He looked exactly like Sylvester the cartoon cat. My heart stopped. My little Tweety Bird was a wobbly flyer at best. One false move and he would be breakfast.

Suddenly a streak of blue plummeted from the sky and attacked the stalking cat. Was it a plane? Was it Superman? No—it was Daddy Bird to the rescue. I laughed in delight as I watched the big blue jay tease and divert the attention of the cat long enough for Mama Bird to get Baby Bird to a higher perch. I smiled, satisfied with the world, as I watched the family fly off together. Sylvester was still lickin' his frustrated chops.

Nature's lesson for me that morning was about letting go and trusting God to use others in his plan for people I love without always assuming I have to be the "Designated Rescuer." I come from a long line of rescuers, pleasers, fixers, and nurturers. Our motto: "If it ain't broke, dive in and fix it anyway!"

I realized this morning that sometimes the only role I need to play in solving most problems is to simply let go, watch, and pray rather than try to force-feed my advice or help.

It is hard to know when and how much to help a friend in need, isn't it? There's a fine line between helping others get on their feet during a crisis, and enabling others, teaching them unhealthy dependency. The Bible tells us to "bear each other's burdens," but it also says "let each man carry his own load." There's a difference between a *burden* and a *load*. One key to knowing when to help is to determine whether your friend is carrying a burden too heavy to carry alone or whether your friend is just refusing to pick up and carry his or her own life's load—the responsibilities we all have to shoulder.

There are times when we absolutely are called to come alongside someone who's been run-over by life in some debilitating way. When one of my dear friends, Carol Kent, found out her only son, an amazing young man, spiritual leader, and graduate of Annapolis Naval Academy had been accused of murder, she was hit with a burden that literally knocked her and her husband, Gene, to their knees.

There's a story in the New Testament about friends who carry their paralytic buddy, who could not walk on his own, to see Jesus to ask for a healing touch. They let him down on a homemade stretcher through the roof of a crowded home, literally delivering him in front of the Christ. Knowing that Gene and Carol would need "stretcher bearers" to help them through unfathomable shock and grief, and the unending legal ordeals ahead, we formed a Stretcher Bearer circle of friends, each of us giving a small portion of time or encouragement, meals or money, cards or small gifts, to help sustain the family through the year before, during, and for a short time after their son's trial. (You can read more about Carol and her son in her poignant memoir, *When I Lay My Isaac Down*.) We helped bear the Kents' burden until their burden became light enough to be a *load* that now Gene and Carol are mostly carrying on their own shoulders, with intermittent help from family and friends.

That's an example of burden-bearing that "fulfills the law of Christ." It's what Christ-followers do for their friends. (I should also mention here, that even as the Kents were bearing their own mountain of pain, when my life began to unravel, they stuck by me like Super Glue, carrying me to Jesus while never leaving my side. What would we do without "Velcro Friends" in this life, people willing to stick with us through the thrill of accomplishment and the agony of crisis?)

On the other hand, we all have situations where we are helping someone who seems to have an unending sense of entitlement. Funny thing, but I recently had another encounter of the bird kind that provided a perfect illustration of this. In my backyard again, I saw an enormous baby bird hopping around the grass, its mouth open wide, chirping like crazy, and waiting for someone to bring him a worm on a silver platter. Then, hilariously, I saw a little bird, half the big guy's size, hop over, and reach UP to pop a worm in Baby Huey's waiting mouth. I still have no explanation for what I saw. Was it a mutant baby bird? Did the mama bird get confused and feed some other bird's giant baby? All I know is the ridiculous sight made me laugh out loud. It was a picture of how many parents feel when they are still feeding and caring for adult children or overly dependent friends who are too lazy to find worms of their own though they are plenty capable of doing so.

How do we help friends or family members who need to start digging for their own worms, so to speak? Years ago, I happened on a wonderfully practical book called *I Don't Have to Make Everything All Better* by Gary and Joy Lundberg. The premise is to help us natural "nurturers" learn to support others in their own self-growth by validation, rather than coming to the rescue and fixing. It promotes saying things like, "I trust you to figure this out. You've got a good mind and a creative spirit!" rather than handing over another check or making another excuse. It's a method that allows you to pour on love and encouragement without enabling. The concept has literally changed my life. I no longer automatically feel obligated to save the world or fix everyone's problems. I evaluate whether my friend (or family member) is carrying a burden or a load. If it is a burden, I ask God what part He'd have me play to help. If it is a load, then I ask God for the right words to validate my friend and her ability to figure out the next right step in her dilemma.

I got a great email from Mary Walker the other day that summed up what I'm trying to say beautifully: "It's not so profound really, being a good friend. It's just figuring out the difference between letting yourself be used by God and choosing to play God. Nothing bothers me more than being hit with the rolled up plan for *somebody else's* life. 'Stick to your own knittin',' my Mom used to say."

Take it from the birds: Letting go is often the only way to allow your loved ones to soar! (And you'll fly a lot lighter, as well.)

❄ ❄ ❄

Look at the birds of the air; they do not sow or reap or store away in barns, and yet your heavenly Father feeds them. Are you not much more valuable than they? Who of you by worrying can add a single hour to his life?

MATTHEW 6:26-27

12

Befriending the Pint-sized

*I expect to pass through life but once.
If therefore, there be any kindness I can
show...let me do it now, and not defer or
neglect it, as I shall not pass this way again.*
WILLIAM PENN

I was in the minor emergency room, with a head-to-toe outbreak of poison ivy, waiting for a doctor to help relieve my agony. As I was waiting, I heard the terrified screams of a young boy in the examining room next door. "Pleeeeeease, Mister Doctor, don't DO that! Don't hurt me! NO! NO! Please, please, please..."

Between the heart-rending pleas, screams, and sobs, I heard enough grownup conversation to surmise that the boy, named Robert, had fallen on a sea shell, cutting his knee deeply. He was in the painful process of getting the wound cleaned, followed by shots for deadening the pain. By the time the ordeal of the first stage was over, the boy, the father, the grandmother, the doctor, the nurse, and all the patients within hearing distance were emotionally spent. I wiped at my own tears, remembering the terror of getting stitches when I was a small child. Suddenly I knew what I had to do.

I rounded the corner, peeked in the curtain and asked if I could talk to the little guy for minute. I quietly explained to the doctor that I wrote children's books, had been a first-grade teacher, and then assured him I spoke fluent Kid-ese. He shrugged his weary shoulders and reluctantly nodded. "You're welcome to give it a try."

The little fellow looked at me, tears streaming, chest heaving. His knee looked as though a small shark had taken a bite out of it. I tried not to wince, and instead looked at the boy's enormous eyes, smiled my friendliest smile, and said, "Hey there, Robert, I couldn't help overhearing all the excitement from next door! What happened to you? And wow, aren't you a BIG BRAVE BOY!" (I decided the best route would be to act "as if.")

What followed was nothing short of a miracle. The boy stopped mid-scream, sniffed a few times, held up his skinny little arm, flexing a muscle the size of walnut and with manly pride exclaimed, "Yeah, and I'm STRONG too!" The doctor blinked in surprise, then asked if I could possibly stay for the remainder of the operation. Robert and I passed the time swapping stories and in a few minutes he was in complete stitches (the laughing kind and the sewing kind). Robert's father, on his knees beside his son, tears standing in his eyes, looked up at me and asked, "Are you an angel?"

And though I could not answer in the affirmative, I do believe I flew home on the wings of the indescribably great feeling of having helped ease a small child's pain in a small way.

I often think of how Jesus welcomed the children to Him, when the disciples were basically trying to shoo the kids away from the Master. To their shock and surprise, and the children's delight, Jesus not only called the kids over to Himself, but He told the grownups around Him that they'd need to become a lot more like these little ones in order to experience God's kingdom realities. (Don't you know at least one of those youngsters must have stuck out his tongue at a smug disciple or two?)

The friends who have meant the most to me over the years have also shown a keen interest in my children. I think the reverse is also true, for "love me, love my kids" is an unstated feeling we all carry around in our hearts.

So make room in your heart for a child-friend or two or more. Shop garage sales and keep a toy closet or box of blocks, games, and coloring books to welcome any children who might come visiting in your home along with their mom or dad. Keep a small table and chair set tucked away or under a bed. Find a special Tippy cup and child-sized plate set. Save some children's books and videos. Stop at the next lemonade stand you see, and donate a quarter to the coffee can bank. Not for the lukewarm Kool-Aid complete with suspicious floaties, but to light up the faces of miniature entrepreneurs. When you meet a family with kids, take just an extra moment to look the kids in the eye and ask a question or two to make them feel special. They are people too. And it doesn't take much kind attention from a grownup for them to feel ten feet tall.

*And whoever welcomes a little child
like this in my name welcomes me.*

MATTHEW 18:5

13

Breathing Lessons

I was in a bathroom stall, hiding out. I was professionally dressed in my pink-and-black "speakers suit" but felt like a formal fish out of water. During my dark night of the soul, the last thing I felt like doing was spreading sunshine and joy to a crowd of women waiting to be inspired and entertained. Besides, what did I have to say? "Lord," I prayed silently, "I dread having to take the stage and the microphone tonight. Let me know you can still use me somehow. I feel like damaged goods with nothing significant to say anymore."

Just then, another woman entered the stall next to mine. I thought I heard coughing and swallowing, and then it got eerily quiet. Except that she began banging on the wall.

"Are you okay?" I asked. No answer. Just more banging.

I came out of my stall and walked over to hers. I opened the door. The woman was struggling to stand, her face literally turning blue. She was obviously choking on something. Now I have to tell you that if you are in an emergency situation, I am the LAST person you'd want to call. Whenever I saw blood on one of my kids, I would throw a towel in the general direction of the wound and try not to look until I could call over more competent help (like an eight-year-old child with a stronger stomach than mine). Once, after a doctor peeled off layer after layer of my "homemade bandaging"—a clean disposable diaper, a hand towel, a sock, and several paper towels—from my son's badly cut leg, he looked up at me and asked, "Becky, were you trying to smother the wound?"

Anyway, back to the bathroom stall. Do not ask me why, but suddenly I felt enveloped in a sort of other-worldly cocoon of sheer peace. I put my arms around the lady and said softly and calmly, like a nun or a saint with paramedic training, "Everything is going to be fine. And now I'm going to do the Heimlich maneuver on you." I only vaguely remembered the Heimlech from seventh-grade health class, but what did I have to lose? So with both hands in a fist, I firmly pressed up and under her sternum and sure enough, it worked!

Out of her mouth popped a pineapple. Not a WHOLE pineapple, mind you. (Although with our family's propensity for exaggeration it may evolve into that at some point.) But a significant chunk of fruit. The woman gulped in air and flung her arms around my neck. "You saved my life!"

"I did?" I responded.

"Yes! Who ARE you?"

"Actually, I am tonight's inspirational speaker. And I'm supposed to be out on stage about now."

"Well, come with me," she said, "I'm going to introduce you in a big way!"

I'll never forget my one and only introduction as "the woman who just saved my life in the bathroom." She even sent me a picture later of the two us after the ordeal as a memento of my brief moment as heroine.

They say that God whispers in the light, but He shouts in the darkness. In my dark night of the soul, God, with his wild sense of humor, shouted to me: "Darlin' (Yeah, He calls me "Darlin'"), I'm not finished with you yet. You're not allowed to be washed up! There are too many hurting souls in need of resuscitation, and some are in a lot more pain than you are in right now."

T.D Jakes says, "Your ministry is where your misery has been." I believe there is a time for recovering from a trauma, for holing up and hiding away and letting the tears fall where they may. But I don't think it is good to stay in bed one more moment than necessary. Jakes put it this way, "There comes a point when you have received enough help that you are no longer on the critical list. The moment you can get up, it is good to do so. You gain strength by helping others…you will never become a minister as long as you lie in the hospital bed yourself. Get up and help someone else survive what you endured. There are so many people who need the bed you are in. You must give it to them and become a part of the solution instead of the problem. That, within itself, is a therapy."

I read an analogy once that compared Christians to a compost pile that is constantly turning. Everyone takes their turn on the bottom of the heap, and those who are doing well, can reach down and help those on the bottom to come on up to the top. But none of us gets the luxury of staying on top all of the time.

We all take our turn on the bottom of life's pit. The compost pile keeps turning, and the players are constantly changing.

Where are you in the compost heap today? Have you been on the bottom a little too long? Is it time for you to reach out to others, to befriend those who are heading where you have just been? There's no greater therapy than making yourself useful to friends in need by being a friend in deed.

"Your ministry is where your misery has been."

❄   ❄   ❄

When a friend is in trouble, don't annoy him
by asking if there is anything you can do.
Think up something appropriate and do it.

EDGAR WATSON HOWE

14

Love Thy Neighbor

My friend and longtime neighbor Melissa has been my traveling companion on this sometimes painful, oft-times hilarious journey of life. She's Ethel to my Lucy, or Lucy to my Ethel, depending on the occasion. She is the sort of friend who would give you anything you might need if she had it to give. In fact, after we'd been friends for a few years I found out, through casual conversation with some of her family members, that she'd given her kidney to a friend's adopted daughter. By some miracle, Melissa's kidney turned out to be a perfect match, and she saved a child's life with her generosity. But Melissa truly feels she only did what any good person would have done and plays down that sacrificial act of benevolence as "no big deal."

Melissa and I once took an unforgettable mini-vacation to Hollywood, California, together. (Making an extra-long stop at the "I Love Lucy" shop at Universal Studios, of course.) Several scenes flash through my mind even now and bring a smile to my lips. We had a blast at Disneyland (without any of our six kids along!), but an interesting descent down an escalator in an airport is the ride that still cracks me up when I think of it.

Both of us were neck deep in luggage. I do not know what possessed Melissa to do this, but she insisted I go ahead of her. When I reached the bottom of the escalator, I managed to step off with some measure of grace. However, my suitcase was much heavier than I realized and I discovered too late—and to our mutual shock—that I did not have the strength to drag if off with me. There it sat, like an ominous road block, stuck on the bottom step which meant that Melissa had to finish her descent, both her arms wrapped around luggage, by straddling my oversized suitcase and letting it pass between her legs. The only other alternative would have been to trip and fall face forward on the floor. To complete this cartoon-like scenario, I might add, Melissa was wearing a dress. I was absolutely helpless with laughter, unable to speak or even to stand up straight for several minutes. For some reason, it took her a little while longer to appreciate the humor of the scenario.

Yet another *I Love Lucy* episode occurred upon boarding the plane to go home. We'd purchased a dozen huge cinnamon rolls for our children, each one the size of a full-grown cantaloupe and placed them in a paper shopping bag to add to our mounting bulk of baggage. Much to our amazement, as we stepped into the airplane galley, the bag broke loose, releasing the rolls. They looked like a dozen sticky bowling balls gone wild as they veered crazily down the alley and under passenger seats.

"Catch that big one coming toward you!" one flight attendant called out to another. "I got it!" she called back, tossing it to Melissa who, I must say, made a very nice catch. At this point the nervous passengers began reflexively ducking, like seventh-grade dodge ball players fearful of getting pelted.

With everyone's help we gathered our assorted sticky buns from hither and yon, when one man hollered, "Here's another roll!" "Where?" I asked. "Up yonder." Melissa pointed.

"Great," I deadpanned. "When the rolls are called up yonder, I'll be there."

Melissa and I were so close, in heart and in proximity, for so many years, that our children would roam in and out of each other's houses without knocking, comfortable with both abodes as home sweet home. Melissa's son, Josh, was a few years older than Gabe, and for many idyllic summers Josh and Gabe spent every day shooting hoops, fishing, or skiing on the lake where we lived. In fact, all four of my kids, along with Josh and his little sister, Sarah, got along with each other more like siblings than friends. (Although, there was one brief summer when my daughter Rachel and Josh became a bit more than good buddies....But that's another story for another chapter.)

Once, after Melissa and her family had returned from a weekend vacation away, I got a telephone call from her.

"Hey, there. Welcome home. What's up?" I asked.

"You aren't going to believe this one," she said, laughing.

"What's Gabe done now?" I asked, as it seemed that my youngest was always the fodder for the latest outrageous story. In fact, if it weren't for Gabe, I would've never had enough material to fill more than two dozen books of family humor.

"Well, we walked into our house and Gabe nearly shocked us out of our minds. He was standing quite nonchalantly at the kitchen counter, looking through the pantry. When I asked, 'Gabe, what are you doing here?' he ignored my question, and said, 'Melissa, you have got to get to the store. There is no good food in this house.'"

Talk about feeling at home! Melissa loves this story and repeats it many times.

To this day, though Melissa and I now live a thousand miles apart, I still feel like she's my next-door neighbor, second mom to my kids, and partner in mischief and merriment, as well as traveling companion through grief and recovery. Other friends have come and gone. They turned out to be friends for a reason or friends for a season. I believe that Melissa will be that very rare gem: a friend for life.

Lucy and Ethel, next-door friends of the heart, forever.

❋　❋　❋

It takes a long time to grow an old friend.

JOHN LEONARD

15

Saying Goodbye
to a Friend

What wound did ever heal but by degrees?
WILLIAM SHAKESPEARE

They say that hard times often come all at once, in a series of difficulties spanning a relatively short time. In the middle of my marriage dissolving, my neighbor and ultimate mama bear friend, Melissa had to face every mother's unthinkable nightmare. She lost her 19-year-old son, Joshua, who was like a part of our family too. In a freak accident, he drowned in the lake we all lived on and enjoyed so much. Not only was Josh a great friend to my boys, he was my daughter Rachel's first boyfriend. My lovely daughter grieved terribly for the loss of her friend, the first boy she ever loved. I would sit by her in church, and every time the service ended with a chorus "Come just as you are" tears would well up in her soft-brown eyes as she thought of Josh and the way he accepted everyone so easily, just as they were.

She could not seem to get over the hump of grief nor the lumps in her throat. Then one day she sat down and wrote the following story and handed it in for a college assignment. She told me that by putting what had happened into a story, she found a gentle release and the peace she had been seeking in dealing with Josh's death. I read it and had to tell her, "Darlin', you have the gift." "The gift" is the natural ability that the females in our family tree seem to have for putting life's events on paper. They say writing is a way to "taste life twice"—and I have found it is also a way to make some organized sense of life when it gets confusing.

I am so proud and pleased to introduce my readers to my daughter's personal glimpse of the sunshine from God during her year of trial and pain.

Lake of Love, Lake of Tears
by Rachel Praise Rhodes
(Becky's daughter)

I grew up at Club Lake in Greenville, TX, with my family. Right outside our house was the lake, the lake that brought so many wonderful memories and good times. I felt like the lake saw who I really was. When I was happy it saw the smiles, and when I cried it caught my tears. We had the most beautiful view of the sunset from our pier. As the sunset reflected on the water, the sky seemed endless, as if the heavens had opened up to earth.

The lake and the memories made on it had a rippling effect on my life, and I will always treasure each day I spent there. However, as my life went on, the lake's presence took on a different aura as it became something of my past; therefore, I no longer look to the lake to express my feelings, but to something much greater than a mass of water.

I made some wonderful friends while I lived at the lake, but I'll never forget Joshua Gantt. As much as I enjoyed looking over the lake and watching the sun go down, my love for the water could not compare to Josh's enthusiasm. He practically lived on the lake: skiing, swimming, knee boarding, wakeboarding, and anything else he could do in the water.

I met Josh on the bus my fifth-grade school year and his sixth. Before I even knew where his stop was, I hopped in the seat next to him while my girlfriends and I tried to find out everything about the new "oh my gosh-he's-so-CUTE!" boy on the bus. Girls developed a crush on Josh just by the mere sight of him, with his dark hair and skin and a smile so bright and mischievous and warm, along with a good-natured charm that was irresistible. I thought I was going to faint when he said he had just moved to Club Lake, two doors down from my family's home. That crush turned into love as I got to know him. He was not just a good-looking guy, but also caring, outgoing, fun, honest, and loving. Josh and I became close friends throughout the years, while I grew out of my childhood figure into a blossoming teenager. By the end of fifth grade, I already decided I would marry Josh.

Finally, the summer after eighth grade, after an agonizing four years of being just his buddy, we became boyfriend and girlfriend. He gave me my first kiss and one of the best summers ever of my youth. He often took me out on the boat with him and his friend

Paul, and on days when Paul did not come, he even trusted me to pull him on his wakeboard, a sport he was quickly mastering.

I remember watching him with awe; he was naturally talented at so many things and so patient with my natural ability to be so bad at so many things. He tried to teach me how to wakeboard several times, but I never could stand up on it; I always ended up looking like a little drowning duck. That summer he was also developing his love for music. He had a guitar and amp and spent hours strumming and singing. He again tried to teach me a few tunes on the guitar, which I slaughtered.

As the summer ended, so did our relationship as a couple. I spent a full 24 hours in tears. I went to the pier and cried my little heart out into the lake, but as most 14 year olds do, I moved on. However, Josh never left my heart. As I dated my next boyfriend, Josh and I still tried to keep our friendship. In letters we both wrote "I love you." Even though it was never actually spoken, we shared a genuine love for each other. I have never questioned for a second my affection for Josh…or his for me. When we saw each other and gave one another a simple hello and a smile, it was always clear that we cared for each other.

My junior year of high school our families spent Thanksgiving together. Josh and I snuck off together and snuggled on the couch at his house and watched a movie, just like we had done several times a few years earlier. He leaned over and kissed me and whispered, "I missed that." We both missed each other, but our lives, by then, were pointing in such different directions. Josh knew that he wasn't meant to be the love of my life. As I talked to his mom, she told me that he felt that he was not the right one for me. Josh always thought of others first. If continuing something risked hurting someone else, he wouldn't take the risk.

Josh never wanted to hurt me, and although sometimes not being his girlfriend did hurt, maybe he somehow knew that my heart would not be able to handle what was to come in his future if I were with him. I would need someone to help me through the trials ahead, and Josh could not be that person.

Josh did know what was best for me, and as I walked out of my bridal cottage last June, he was the first person I saw standing in front of me. We locked eyes and smiled at each other. The look on his face was one of beaming pride, as if he had been waiting his whole life to see me happily married. He had known all along that the perfect guy would come and sweep me away.

That was the last day I saw Josh.

At about six o'clock, as I lay in bed with my husband in my new home in Tyler, I was awakened by a phone call from my dad.

"Sweetie, we lost Josh Gantt last night. He got caught in some fishing line and drowned. I'm so sorry."

"God...no," was all I could say.

I thought of Josh's family—his parents, his sister, his grandparents, all of whom were good friends to me and my family. How their hearts would be breaking! I quickly got ready and drove home to Club Lake to be with the family. Trying to hold back tears, I had to go someplace where I could yell and cry and break down. So I headed to the Gantts' pier, by the lake where Josh and I grew up together, now the lake that took his life. Still the lake caught my tears and the peaceful wake comforted me.

I did not realize it at the time, but now I understand that there was Someone else with me who was sharing my pain, yet rejoicing over the new life Joshua was beginning. In my mind's eye, I'm sitting by the lake crying, while these big, strong arms are wrapped around me and a gentle kiss brushes my forehead. It is the warm presence of God. I've caught my breath and the pain eases just a little bit at a time. Over the next year this Presence will not leave my side and He, simply by hovering so close to my heart, lessens a little bit of the pain one day at a time.

❋   ❋   ❋

I, even I [the Lord your Maker],
am he who comforts you.

Isaiah 51:12

16

Feathers from Heaven

Hope is the thing with feathers on it.
EMILY DICKINSON

Years ago my friend Melissa was driving along one day, when she reached over and found a white feather attached to her shoulder. She picked it off, smiled, turned to her husband Michael and said, "Look what my angel left me." They shared a good laugh and drove on, not giving the incident much thought.

A couple of years later Melissa was at the funeral of her grandmother when her husband said, "Look on your shoulder." He pointed to a white feather that had somehow landed there. Not long after this second feather experience, Melissa found herself in the emergency room. Her little girl, Sarah, was being examined for a head injury after hitting her head on a dock in a waterskiing accident. Melissa was afraid, as any mother would be, and every breath was a prayer. When she and Michael were allowed in to see their daughter, there on the sheet, was a feather.

Michael, normally not a sentimental man, took the white feather that had found its way to his daughter's bedside and later brought it to the car and put it in a special box as a keepsake from above. All would be well, both in Melissa's heart and, thankfully, with Sarah's head. (She's since had yet another head injury and subsequent visit to the emergency room after falling off a golf-cart onto concrete. We tell her she's blessed to be hard-headed.)

As you read in the previous chapter, Sarah lost her big brother Josh this year. The loss is too big to contain in words; however, since the day Joshua left earth for heaven, it has been raining feathers.

There was one large, white feather stuck to the front door of the Gantts' home the morning after Josh died. I was with Melissa on a trip to Montana several months afterward, a girlfriend get-away to do some healing and have some fun, when, just before we left to go home, I saw Melissa reach down and pull a white feather from the top of her suitcase. "I have a stack of them now. I find them everywhere," she explained. "And Josh's girlfriend called to tell me she came back to her desk at work today to find two white feathers in her chair."

On one particularly hard day, not long after Josh died, Melissa allowed Sarah to stay home from school. My friend held her daughter as she cried and grieved convulsions of sorrow that went with missing her brother. Then Sarah wiped her tears, stood up, and headed toward the kitchen for a drink of water. "Sarah," Melissa said, laughing through her tears. "Look at the seat of your pants."

Sure enough there was a white feather attached to Sarah's

behind. "That would be just like Josh," she said, one hand on her hip, and then she smiled for the first time that day.

At a later time I was standing in front of a mirror in a hotel room, far from my Texas home, when I happened to notice a white feather stuck to the front of my shirt. Half-joking, half-wondering, I said aloud, "Josh? Lord? Anything you two want to say to us today?" I said it spontaneously, with a chuckle in my voice, but I remember the incident clearly because I spoke the question aloud, even though I was alone. Though I would never claim to be altogether normal, I don't usually talk to myself out loud.

That afternoon I flew home and met my son Gabe for dinner. Before we had barely settled into the restaurant booth he said, "Mom, I woke up from the weirdest, but best dream about Joshua this morning."

"Really?" I asked, more curious because of my own fine-feathered experience that day. "Tell me about it."

"Well," he said, "I dreamed I was walking along the lakeside road and Josh came walking toward me. I knew it was a dream, and I knew Josh was in heaven and I was still on earth, but I could talk to him. So I asked him, 'Josh, what is God like?' And Joshua said, 'You know, Gabe, God is a lot more down to earth than we thought.'"

Yes, I thought, *I believe that. Now more than ever.* In fact, He may be close enough to let a feather fall from His hand onto our sagging shoulders.

I don't know if the feathers we are finding are truly heavenly signs of comfort. I'll concede (but not without some protest) that this could all be coincidence.

I also don't know if Gabe's dream was anything more than a dream. How could I prove what will remain a mystery until the veil of this life has been lifted? Until we discover, someday, what has truly been going on behind the scenes of the days of our lives, no human being can speak authoritatively on "coincidences" around us. The Bible only explains enough to reassure us there is a fascinating life beyond death, more wonderful than we can possibly imagine, but the description is just vague enough to leave plenty of room for myriad surprises.

Who knows? Perhaps one of the mysteries solved in heaven someday will be bumping into a ministering angel whose job it was to look for people whose hearts were heavy-laden—and lighten them with feathers.

❉ ❉ ❉

Life isn't measured by how many breaths you take, but how often life takes your breath away.

AUTHOR UNKNOWN

17

Soulmates, Playmates

"This is my beloved...this is my friend."
Song of Solomon 5:16 nkjv

I bought a greeting card for myself the other day. I simply couldn't resist because the photo and caption sums up who I am today. There's a little girl, about age four, on the front of the card. She's looking up tentatively, hopefully, her hands open to receive some drops of fresh spring rain. The caption says, "Then just when we think we'll never smile again...life comes back."

In an earlier chapter I wrote about losing myself as the puzzle pieces of my life blew up in the agony and aftermath of divorce. Just when I thought I'd never smile again, never be cherished, wanted, loved, or held—a seven-year friendship was set on fire. Respect turned to romance, like turned to love, and Greg Johnson and I, two lonely souls, became one in holy matrimony.

More recently Greg and I were headed out for a little week-long getaway with each other. In fact, as we were going through (or should I say "flirting our way through") the airport security gate, one guard asked if we were just married. After nearly two years, we're still in honeymoon glow. Strangers often comment about how happy we look, and what a joy it is to see a married couple so in love. (I'm sure what they aren't saying is, "especially at your ages.") One day we were walking along the beach, and an ancient-looking old woman looked at us, smiled, paused, and just started serenading us—quite out of the blue—with the song "Amoré." Another evening after a romantic dinner at our favorite Italian restaurant, we strolled outside and danced to the music just as a young waitress passed by. She said, "You two are just too cute." With Italian music playing out over the sidewalk and to the parking lot, Greg held me close to his heart, gently kissed my forehead, and said, "I want to be too cute forever."

We are high on our newfound love and, apparently, it shows. Ours is a true friendship set on fire with passion beyond anything either of us have ever known. We knew each other, platonically, for seven years. And though we had complete respect and admiration for each other, never in a thousand years did we imagine that someday we'd end up married. But here we are, like peas 'n' carrots, inseparable best friends as well as lovers. What a deal this is! We both get misty-eyed fairly regularly, with the wonder of finding such a soulmate/playmate at midlife.

For our first year of marriage we worked and played. I cooked, and we ate (growing plump on home-cooked meals and happiness). We enjoyed spontaneous "bathtub" board meetings. We flirted and flitted our days away—just the two of us. "You make me feel so young! You make me feel there are songs to be sung!"

seemed to be the theme song pulsing through our veins and our home. We're almost 50, going on 18. Though Greg and I both work at home in a literary business, he downstairs and I in my upstairs office, we often e-mail each other with flirtations and sweet nothings in-between editorial suggestions and client-related questions.

In Jewish law, a young man was required to stay home for the first year of his marriage to "make his wife happy." After spending a low-key, low-stress year together working, living, and loving each other 24/7 side-by-side, I am all for reinstating this law. It makes for a fabulous foundation for a new marriage as you get to really know one another's little routines, habits, charms, and flaws. As Greg says, "We're getting our Ph.D. in each other."

One classic example of my husband learning how to Operate a Becky happened in our first few months of marriage. For some reason, I have developed a decades-long habit of leaving lids off things. This means that at any moment the milk or the mustard, or both, may be uncapped and gelling in the fridge. Greg, preferring his milk not taste like mustard or yesterday's tuna, requested I try harder to remember to put on lids and avoid tossing them in the trash. I promised to try. And I was very pleased with myself as I noticed that the milk was nearly always capped when I checked the fridge. Mentioning this to Greg, I said, "See? You can teach an old dog new tricks." Greg smiled and shook his head. "Or you can trick an old dog." With that he opened a drawer and showed me his lid collection.

"What's this?" I asked, bewildered.

"I couldn't get you to remember to replace caps so I decided to just adjust to the situation. I started saving extra lids and when you throw one away, I just quietly replace it without saying anything. It's no big deal. It's not a character flaw. You make me happy in a hundred other more important ways."

Greg's also learned that I make no sense at all until after I have had coffee (which he often brings me in bed), and even after I'm fully caffeinated, conversations with me can still be interesting. I've not a blond hair on my brunette head, but I think I've accumulated more "blond moments" than Ellie May Clampett and Jessica Simpson combined.

Just the other night we spotted the famous poker champion, Amarillo Slim, on an ESPN channel. Back in the days before Texas Hold 'Em was cool, Greg's father was a professional poker player and won an Amarillo Slim Poker Tournament so I was fascinated to see this icon in the flesh. "Wow," I said, noting Slim's Southern drawl and ten gallon hat. "He must be from Texas."

"You think so?" Greg asked.

"Yeah, he's probably from West Texas somewhere, I think, judging by that accent of his."

"Well," Greg said with a wink, "I don't think he's from Tyler or Dallas."

"Hmmm…maybe he's from Sweetwater, where my parents are from!" I mused aloud.

"Becky," Greg said kindly, "do you think there's any chance at all that since his name is Amarillo Slim he might be from *Amarillo?*"

"Oh…duh, "I said, smiling sheepishly. "Greg, I can't believe I didn't catch that. Do you wonder about my brain sometimes?"

"It's not a character flaw, Sweetie," he said, his eyes shining with a mixture of amusement and love. "You're cute and that's all that matters."

On our way back home from our little vacation last week,

we were going through the metal detector at the airport again. I was asked to remove my belt because of the buckle. Little could anyone have known how hard I had to work that morning to get my belt shoved into the almost-too-tight loops. And now the belt simply wasn't budging. I was holding up the line with my struggle, so I turned around and looked helplessly at Greg and said, "Sir? Would you mind helping me with my belt?" To the raised eyebrows and shocked faces of guards and passengers behind us in line, Greg poked and prodded and tugged and pulled at my belt, hugging me tight to get a better grip now and then. Finally one guard couldn't take the suspense any longer. "Lady, do you even *know* this man?"

Greg and I grinned at each other and at what people around us must have been thinking. I finally admitted, "Yeah, I know him. Actually I know him in the *biblical sense* of the word."

God's sense of humor at work: Greg, who has always lived a quiet, fairly predictable life, has ended up with a wife who is anything but predictable. Even going through a security gate becomes an "experience." I've made his once-ordered life messy in a dozen different ways, but he reassures me the laughter and affection that go with the mess is totally worth the trouble. He is kindness personified in his unconditional acceptance of me just as I am.

I have a little plaque in the kitchen that says, "Love, like bread, must be made fresh every day." It is amazing how quickly a good love can slip away if one or both neglect the other for even a short period of time. God's given Greg and me a second chance at love, a second chance at life, and we are determined to cherish this gift.

On their fiftieth anniversary this last Christmas, my father lovingly sang to my mother the beautiful song, "Forever Is as Far as I'll Go." There wasn't a dry eye in our living room as Greg and I, along with my siblings and our children, watched the beautiful scene play out. My parents are a rare couple—soulmates and playmates, and very best friends.

Greg and I know that true, long-lasting love like this is rare. We're acutely aware that it only happens by loving each other as deeply, as kindly, and as often as you can every single day, in some way. It means honoring your friendship with tender courtesies and keeping a sharp eye out for opportunities to fan the flames of passion (like going through an airport metal detector). It's the only way we can stay "too cute forever" until our own fiftieth anniversary...when we'll be almost 100 years young, going on 18.

This morning my husband shared some correspondence between my parents and him that occurred just this week as Greg celebrated his fiftieth birthday and we heralded our second anniversary. I think it is as telling as anything I might say about my husband's ability to "love a Becky" and my parents joy as they watch my life...come back (along with showcasing their natural gift of encouragement—part of the reason they have a long line of loving friends and family surrounding them).

Dear Greg,

If we were a little younger, we'd be turning cartwheels this morning over all God's done in and through you. We marvel not only at God's love for you, but at your ability to succeed so well in your field.

And, along with that, to love and cherish and keep up with our extra-special little girl, along with all the young'uns you two have between you.

Know we love you,
George & Ruthie

Dear George and Ruthie:

Thank you so much for rejoicing with me. It's fun to have a few cheerleaders.

And thanks for your birthday greetings.

On Sunday it will be two years since I married your lovely daughter. She's my light, my heart, my truest love. Marriage works when two people are committed to each other as much as we are…it works the way it should—wonderfully.

God is taking care of our little business, and I'm more than excited about taking care of your daughter all of her days. There is lots to worry about in life, but you can take worrying about Becky off your list. Husbanding her is a challenge at times, but always a joy, never a burden.

Thanks for raising such a wonderful woman.

Love,
Greg

Dear Son-in-Law,

What a fantastic letter. Thanks for all the lovely things you said about Becky and your life with her. I think I do have a pretty good understanding of how you feel about her and how much you enjoy living with her, even with its interesting challenges.

She kept us smiling and laughing from day one, but especially as she began to blossom into a teenager. The other two kids would finish dinner and leave the table, but often Becky would stay at the table, sit in one or the other of our laps, and just CLOWN! Talk about charm...

But she was and is so much more than that—very tender of heart, sensitive, and smart. She does, however, need somebody to stay handy and catch the debris, find the treasured object she needs, stay in good humor, and just generally enable her to shine her light and do all the lovely things she does best.

Every day we thank God for her and also for the one to whom the Father has given the above assignment.

With love,
George and Ruthie

If you are married today, how seriously are you taking your God-given assignment to supportively love and encourage your mate? Applauding his (or her) gifts, gently helping him with his weaknesses, cherishing him just because this precious soul is your sacred trust? Willy Nelson sings an old, sad song about a love that was "always on his mind"—and yet the songwriter recounts all the ways he neglected to show his love or shower his mate with the words she so needed to hear—until it was too late.

Dear reading friend, don't let the love in your mind and heart go unspoken. Tend well and with regularity the many loves of your life. Water your marriage with words of warmth and passion. Give a cheerleading blessing to a child, whether he or she is 2 or 20 or 50. Share the sunshine of your smile with a friend today, whether that friend is a stranger you meet on a crowded street or a special "kindred spirit and bosom buddy" you've cherished for decades.

Yes, love is like bread. Regularly knead in the yeast of human kindness to all your relationships, and you'll never want for a warm hand to hold should your world turn suddenly dim and cold.

❋ ❋ ❋

If two lie down together, they will keep warm.
But how can one keep warm alone?

ECCLESIASTES 4:11

Love is friendship set on fire.

JEREMY TAYLOR

18

Big Hair Blessin's

---

*It is one of the blessings of old friends that
you can afford to be stupid with them.*

RALPH WALDO EMERSON

My sister and I agreed to join my old friend, Suzanne, along
with a couple of her best gal pals, for a weekend girlfriend getaway
deep in magnolia country. Suzanne's husband, Garth, had been my
pastor years ago in Texas at Pleasant Grove Baptist Church #2—
though for the life of me, I couldn't figure out what the "#2" stood
for since our town was so tiny there was room for only one Baptist
church. (And this in a state where we have more Baptist churches
per capita than Kentucky Fried Chickens and Krispy Kremes
combined.) Garth and Suzanne now lived and ministered in the
picturesque southern town of Barnesville, Georgia, surrounded
by a congregation of slow-talking, sweet-tea-brewing, fried-green-
tomato-eating, gracious and kindly parishioners.

So there we were one summer day—Suzanne, my sister, and I, in Suzanne's car—packed and ready for the two-hour road trip to Callaway Gardens in Pine Mountain, Georgia. But first we had to stop to meet and greet Suzanne's friend, Maureen. We pulled up in front of a tan-and-white storybook cottage so charming I half-expected the gingerbread man to come running out the door.

As the driver and designated door knocker, Suzanne stepped out of the car and scooted up the porch to fetch Maureen. Maureen was not only Suzanne's neighbor and confidante, she was her hairdresser—or, as Maureen preferred to be called, her "glamor technician." Rach and I had been silently hoping Suzanne would show good taste in choosing the other gals who would be joining us on our mini-vacation.

When Maureen opened the front door, she didn't just walk down the steps—she *sashayed* down them on clouds of giggles. Rachel leaned over from her place in the front seat, gave me a knowing wink, and said with audible relief, "She looks like our kind of gal." I nodded in eager agreement.

Maureen's hair was a perfectly coiffed ball of blond fluff. Scarlet lipstick outlined a smile as welcoming as a Southern summer morning. Her bountiful figure epitomized the word *voluptuous*. She smelled of honeysuckle and apple blossoms. If there had been a theme song to accompany Maureen's stroll down the sidewalk runway and into our lives, I'm sure it would have been "I Enjoy Being a Girl."

The first words out of her bright-red lips completed the charming picture. "Don't ya'll just know this trip is going to be such a blessin'?"

Since our car was already bulging at the seams, Maureen

and Susan (Suzanne's other friend and a Delta flight attendant) decided to take their own vehicle, with our threesome following close behind. As we drove among emerald hills and adorable country towns, we watched in amazement the drama playing out in the car in front of us. Red fingernails flying, blond hair bobbing, two mouths that never closed. Astounding how Southern women can talk, listen, let the paint on their nails dry, and drive a vehicle all at the same time.

I glanced around at Suzanne and Rachel and realized that all of us were visibly straining toward the car in front of us, as if by leaning forward enough we could catch the good pieces of gossip flying between Maureen and Susan.

Exhausted from the long flight from Texas to Atlanta earlier that day, I soon fell asleep in the backseat. I came to consciousness only after I felt the car come to a complete stop and heard the excitement of the four newly released women—sprung, as it were, from their black-and-white routines into a vacation of living color.

First stop: quaint religious bookstore.

"To see if they have your books, Hon," Maureen said, poking her head through the backseat window. I gave her a sleepy, questioning look.

While they chatted among themselves, I scrounged for my makeup bag to no avail. Finally giving up, I tagged behind the waddling, cackling gaggle of women. As soon as we hit the bookstore, we dispersed—me to look for a mirror, the others to check out the book stock.

"Excuse me," said Maureen, flashing her brilliant smile at the unsuspecting clerk, "but do you have any books by Becky Freeman? Because you see, she's OUR friend and a WON-derful writer." (This took place several years before my remarriage and "Johnson" was added to my byline.)

"Hmmm…I may have one," said the clerk nonchalantly. "Look ovuh they-uh."

I breathed a sigh of relief when I saw that at least mine wasn't on the dreaded bargain table or clearance shelf. There I was, instead, on a revolving paperback rack—in living print.

Now can we go? I wanted to ask. *Why is it I'm always caught without makeup and dressed in an old sweatshirt whenever I'm called upon to act famous?* I wondered.

Too late. The clerk held a copy the book in her hand, flipped it over, and examined the photo on the back. My *glamor* photo, no less. She looked at me, in all my disheveled reality, then back at the book and declared flatly. "This picture don't look nothin' like you."

I don't know why I didn't just say, "You're right. It isn't. We were just playing a little joke on you," and be done with it. But I have this deeply bred Southern trait: I want people to like me, to believe me, and—if at all possible—to love and cherish me. If I were a homeless person, my hand-lettered cardboard sign would read: *Will Work for Approval.*

"Somebody hand me a tube of lipstick—quick," I whispered.

My sister obliged.

I slid the color over my lips while Maureen wordlessly went straight to work poufing my hair with her long fingernails and deftly shellacking a couple of loose strands in place with her pocket-size bottle of Stiff Spritz. (Big-haired women in humid climates do not go anywhere without their mega-hold hairspray.)

Then Susan, Suzanne, and Rachel took turns holding the book with my picture on it beside my authentic face.

"See the resemblance now?" Maureen asked hopefully.

"Just ignore that little upholstery pattern on her right cheek," my sister added. "Becky was napping in the car."

The clerk looked at the book once more, then back at me, and made her final judgment. "Don't look like you."

"Well," I wearily responded, "right now I don't feel like me either. I need a good jolt of caffeine. Is there a soda machine anywhere around here?"

She jerked her head toward the front porch. I went outside and scrounged up enough quarters for a cold drink in the recesses of my purse. Since I was in hillbilly country, I pressed the dispenser button for a Mountain Dew. After taking a long, refreshing swig, I looked up just in time to see the rest of the belles walking out of the store in a protective huff.

"Well, I never!" said Maureen as she gave me a sideways squeeze. "That clerk was downright rude. Didn't know what she was talkin' about. What? Was she BLIND? That picture looks just like you, Sweetie."

"I thought you perked up real nice once you put on the lipstick," my sister added thoughtfully, "and rubbed the seat cushion pattern out of your face."

"I smell barbecue," said Suzanne.

I was supremely grateful for the change of topic.

We walked across the cobblestone street to a country-style road stand and ordered three barbecue sandwiches to split between the five of us—just a snack to tide us over until we got to our condominium in the mountains.

As we sat around the picnic table in the warm, late-afternoon sun, Maureen let go with one of her famous laughs, looked at me, and said, "Well, it's a blessin', Darlin', that you have such a good sense of humor. Lots of women would be cryin' now over that lady's insultin' remarks."

"Oh," I smiled back, wiping spicy red sauce from my chin. "It's all material. You watch, this episode will probably end up in a book somewhere, sometime."

Maureen offered a final consolation prize, giving her famous benediction once more with feeling, "Honey, you're such a *blessin'!*"

Over the next few days together, we gals would discover that most pleasant things—from a good laugh, to a soft rain, to high cheekbones, to those "cute little specks of sage in the dressin' "—were all *blessin's* to Maureen.

But the biggest blessin' of all, to me, was the chore-free, guilt-free, chick-chat-filled, empathy-loaded, laugh-out-loud time of female bonding. With all those Georgia accents floating on the breeze, I kept having the oddest feeling that we were on the set of *Steel Magnolias,* with Maureen playing Dolly Parton's benevolent beautician role to absolute perfection.

Other than the love of God and family, is there anything more precious than a flock of fun friends who love you just as you are, who believe you to be both famous and glamorous even when you are, in actuality, barely known and wearing an imbedded upholstery pattern where your golden-beige foundation and peach blush should be?

I saw a greeting card once that had a picture of southern women gathered together having a great time, their hair teased and sprayed to excessive heights. The caption declared, "The bigger the hair, the closer to God."

I, for one, believe it. Praise the Lord…and pass the spritz.

❋   ❋   ❋

May God be gracious to us and bless us
and make his face shine upon us.

PSALM 67:1

19

Eight Things I've Learned About Friendship

(with a little backup from other great minds)

1. **It is better to have one or two close friends than a huge network of friendly acquaintances.**

   *True happiness consists not in the
   multitude of friends,
   but in their worth and choice.*

   BEN JONSON

   *True friendship is a plant of slow growth, and
   must undergo and withstand the shocks of
   adversity before it is entitled to the appellation.*

   GEORGE WASHINGTON

2. Until a friendship is tested by the fire of personal failure and outside adversity; a sudden success and a heartbreaking loss—it is still too soon to declare someone your "lifelong friend."

A friend is one who walks in when others walk out.

WALTER WINCHELL

A friend is someone who is there for you when he'd rather be anywhere else.

LEN WEIN

Anybody can sympathise with the sufferings of a friend, but it requires a very fine nature to sympathise with a friend's success.

OSCAR WILDE

3. To be a good friend, let God do the judging, you focus on the loving. Only God knows another's heart, background, chemical make-up, and their log of past life experiences. How much richer your friendships will be if you use your small time on earth to love them, rather than trying to figure them out or correct them.

If you judge people, you have no time to love them.

MOTHER TERESA

Every man should have a fair-sized cemetery in which to bury the faults of his friends.

HENRY BROOKS ADAMS

When we honestly ask ourselves which person in our lives means the most to us, we often find that it is those who, instead of giving much advice, solutions, or cures, have chosen rather to share our pain and touch our wounds with a gentle and tender hand. The friend who can be silent

with us in a moment of despair or confusion,
who can stay with us in an hour of grief and
bereavement, who can tolerate not knowing, not
curing, not healing and face with us the reality of
our powerlessness, that is a friend who cares.

HENRI NOUWEN

4. When you've spent time with a real friend—you'll feel refreshed, encouraged, and occasionally, lovingly challenged. If you've spent time with someone who says he or she is your friend but leaves you feeling somehow less-then, not as special, or emotionally drained—you may admire this person's fine qualities, but the person is not a true friend.

My best friend is the one who
brings out the best in me.

HENRY FORD

Friendship is born at that moment when
one person says to another: "What! You,
too? Thought I was the only one."

C.S. LEWIS

5. Friends I enjoy most share their heart and also listen on a deeper-than-average level in conversation. Also, the conversation is a nice, balanced trade-off of give and take, listening and sharing.

Everyone hears what you say. Friends
listen to what you say. Best friends
listen to what you don't say.

AUTHOR UNKNOWN

6. Friends who love to laugh simply make my day. They don't have to be comedians (in fact, this can get old), but simply be connoisseurs of the funny, quirky, oddly humorous side of life.

Among those whom I like or admire, I can find
no common denominator, but among those
whom I love, I can: all of them make me laugh.

W.H. AUDEN

7. Friends know the secret of staying connected without smothering. There's an easy intimacy of soul and sincerity of caring—with lots of freedom attached. A delightful friendship is always knowing your presence is wanted and welcome, but an understanding that both need times of space and solitude and a full life beyond your friendship.

"Stay" is a charming word in a friend's vocabulary.

LOUISA MAY ALCOTT

Do not allow yourself to be imprisoned by any
affection. Keep your solitude. The day, if it ever
comes, when you are given true affection there
will be no opposition between interior solitude
and friendship, quite the reverse. It is even by
this infallible sign that you will recognize it.

SIMONE WEIL

8. Real friendship allows you to trade roles with ease—one day you're down and in need of a shoulder to lean on. The next day your shoulder is the one getting soggy.

The best friendships are seesaws. Sometimes
you are down, and she's up. Sometimes
he's up and you're down. What makes the
partnership fun—is fairly equal back and
forth, give-and-take quality of the play.

BECKY JOHNSON

20

The Friend You've Always Dreamed Of

═══════════════════════════════════

I have called you friends.
JOHN 15:15

A few years ago, I wrote the following experience in a book that is now out of print. Little did I realize how often I would cling to the memory of this dream in lonesome and frightening seasons to come.

For about a decade, I would speak often at women's spiritual retreats, and many times I'd close by sharing a reading of this essay. However, I was never able to finish it without my voice breaking from the sweet emotion of the memory, along with my heart's longing to experience this sort of all-embracing presence again. Even as I read it again today I realize how words fail to capture the miraculous feeling of being overcome by unconditional love. Women would sometimes write me afterward and ask for a copy so they could read it again for themselves, a reminder of God's tender companionship in difficult hours.

To feel both fully known and fully cherished is perhaps the greatest joy a person can know—and I think this may very well be what makes heaven, well...*heaven*.

I'd like to share it once more as a benediction to this book. May it bless you as it has blessed me.

❄   ❄   ❄

I'm much more of a daydreamer than a night dreamer, but I once had a night dream so vivid and so real that I woke up feeling as if I'd gone away and come back to earth with a bit of heaven tucked in the palm of my hand. Whether it was just a dream that was symbolic to me personally or a gift-dream from the Lord's heart to my soul, I do not know. I share it with you as one who is wary of people who say "God told me this" or "The Lord gave me a dream." However, I'm also a person who believes that in unexpected moments God does indeed give His children personal glimpses of Himself, His goodness, His merciful nature. It's the way of a good friend to do that on occasion. This was my dream...

> I was walking along a beach barefooted when a young man with dark, curly hair came up and asked me to dance. I assumed by his looks that he was Italian.
>
> "But I have no shoes," I told him. "Will you walk with me back to the house so I can get them?"
>
> And as we walked along the beach, I looked into his eyes and

had the strangest feeling that I was looking at someone who knew me better than I knew myself. He had the wisdom of a father, the easy camaraderie of a brother or close friend, and the intimate knowing of my naked soul like a loving husband.

The longer we talked, the more at ease I was in the presence of such kindness and acceptance and the more I felt completely myself. He was the sort of person who invited one's shoulders to relax, one's words to flow freely, unchecked by self-consciousness.

We passed by all the people I knew and loved the most—my parents, my children, my husband—and I waved to each of them, introducing them to my friend.

When we arrived in front of my house, I asked my friend if he was Italian.

"No," he said, with a soft smile. "I'm Jewish."

I nodded and then turned to go get my shoes.

"Wait," he said, holding out his arms. "You'll not need your shoes to dance with Me."

"I looked into those incredible eyes once again, and then I caught my breath—for I knew He was no ordinary man. And, indeed, there was no need for shoes because I was standing on holy ground.

I awoke from that dream, but I've never been quite the same since. I had been in the presence of someone who saw me as I really was, only He filtered everything—the good, bad, and ugly—through His eyes of love.

In my dream, I waltzed with the Friend of friends, the Lover of my soul, under the very stars He had once flung into space. And now, even in the light of day, I dream of the time I will lean on the everlasting arms again, dancing to the music of angels, lost in the warmth of His love.

❄ ❄ ❄

Were not our hearts burning within us while he talked with us on the road?

Luke 24:32

From Becky Freeman Johnson...

❋ ❋ ❋

With my new marriage and a nearby (and ever-growing) passel of children-turned-adults, I've taken on lots of happy new roles: wife, mom, mother-in-law, stepmom, and grandmother. I also support my husband, Greg, in his literary business with editing, client support, and hostessing.

Because of these wonderful changes and the time it takes to be available to my family, I rarely do public speaking. However, if you need a good speaker for your event, may I recommend my good friends Gene and Carol Kent at Speak Up Speaker Services? They can be contacted at www.speakupspeakerservices.com.

For updates on my books and other news or information visit me at

www.yellowroseeditorial.com

It's Fun to Be Your Friend

When lives intersect and a bond between women is formed, the treasures of faithfulness, loyalty, and authenticity are discovered. Becky reflects on all these gifts and more as she shares joy-filled stories about how a cherished friend knows us better than we know ourselves, extends forgiveness and grace, believes in our goodness and gifts, offers silence or conversation when we need it, and becomes a reflection of unconditional love.

It's Fun to Be Your Sister

In this gathering of delightful stories about the connection between sisters and sisters-of-the-heart, each engaging chapter reveals why a sister is the gift that keeps on giving. Women with sisters are able to laugh more at life and at themselves, rest in what they have in common, find blessings and inspiration in each other, walk through life with joy and laughter, and share the biggest trials and the simplest pleasures.

It's Fun to Be a Mom

Becky invites women to take a break, catch their breath, and savor stories of pure joy about the privilege, the labor, and the gift of motherhood. These engaging, short tales lead moms to embrace the habits of highly real moms, the strange miracle of breast feeding, the loss of brain cells when one gains a child, the quest for sleep and romance after kids, and the amazing strength of their own mothers.

It's Fun to Be a Grandma

A grandma is to be revered and celebrated. And Becky does just that with stories from her life as a granddaughter and grandmother. With warmth, insight, and her trademark humor, Becky lifts up these special women who believe wholeheartedly in their children and grandchildren, become the keeper of stories and memories, have incomparable strength of spirit and heart, show the women following them how to live richly, and never tire of talking to or about their grandbabies.